GIRLS' LIFE MAGAZINE

# GL Ask Lucky!
## The Girls' Life Guide to
# Dealing with Dilemmas

Edited by
Kelly White and
Lori Stacy

Illustrated by
Lisa Parett

## Scholastic Inc.
New York • Toronto • London • Auckland • Sydney
Mexico City • New Delhi • Hong Kong • Buenos Aires

ISBN 0-439-44982-0

Design: Mark Neston

12 11 10 9 8 7 6 5                                        7 8/0

Printed in the U.S.A.

First Scholastic printing, August 2003

# CONTENTS

GIRLS' LIFE MAGAZINE

# GL Ask Lucky!
## The Girls' Life Guide to
# Dealing with Dilemmas

# HEY, GIRLS!

**H**i, I'm Lucky! Yep, that's my name. Well, my nickname, anyway. My real name is Alexis, but that was too much of a mouthful for my little brother to say when he was learning to talk—so he called me Lucky instead. And it stuck. Now, everybody knows me as Lucky. And, *you* might know me from my *Girls' Life* advice column, "Ask Lucky."

Girls write to me with their questions, and I give them advice. I'm 17 now, and I've already gone through situations like you might find yourself going through now.

Hopefully, you feel comfortable talking to your family or pals about confusing stuff that occasionally comes with being a girl. But maybe by reading this book, you'll get some extra insight on how to handle just about any situation or—sometimes even better—learn how to prevent potential problems before they even happen.

Inside these pages, you'll find loads of Q&A's on things like friendships, crushes, family, school, and more. Pretty cool, huh? You'll also get the real deal from real girls like you. The tips, topics, and advice are from *Girls' Life* readers who've made some smart moves.

All set? If so, get reading!

*Lucky*

# CHAPTER 1

# FRIENDSHIP FUNDAMENTALS

**M**y friends are super important to me, as I'm sure yours are to you. And in fact, one of the neat things about being a girl is all the great friendships that are formed with other girls—pals you can share just about anything with.

But, how do you find all those great friends in the first place, and what do you do when trouble strikes even your truest friendships?

# FINDING FRIENDS

I know that making friends isn't always as easy as it sounds. Some friendships just seem to form on their own, like when you get seated next to a really great girl in class and the two of you hit it off from day one, or when you just happen to live around the corner from your BFF. But other friendships require extra effort. Here are some tips for getting to know new girls and forming friendships.

*Dear Lucky,*

*I've been trying to make friends with some popular girls. What's the best way to approach them?*

*—On the Outside*

It's great to venture out and make new friends. But it's also important to make new friends for the right reasons—not just because the girls you want to be friends with are popular or whatever. It isn't cool to use people because of who they are or what they have. So, assuming you genuinely dig these girls, here's the scoop: Instead of approaching the whole crew at once, strike up one-on-one conversations—at your lockers, in the lunch line, or before gym class. Initiate chit-chat by bringing up something you have in common—like Mr. Yawn's sleep-inducing tirades on Civil War cannons in social studies. Don't think about that girl in the lunch line as "popular"— approach her like a friend. Say something like, "Oh, super. It's meatloaf in the caf...*again*." If she laughs or pipes in, consider the ice broken. Then, test the waters and offer to save her a seat at the best people-watching table. Maybe some of her buds will join you, too. If so, ask if anyone's up for a history study session in the a.m. Take small steps, and don't be discouraged if you don't become BFFs with everyone overnight. You can't rush friendships, but you *can* make new friends!

## SASHA SAID IT!

### MAKING NEW FRIENDS

Are you starting a new school? Are you new to a friend-infused neighborhood? What?! Think you can't make some new pals? Here's a checklist to making-new-friends success! Don't forget to:

1. Act nicely

2. Strike up conversations

3. Ask questions to discover what you might have in common with others

4. Be interesting

5. Be positive

6. Plan a get-together

7. Act like yourself

—Sasha G., 13

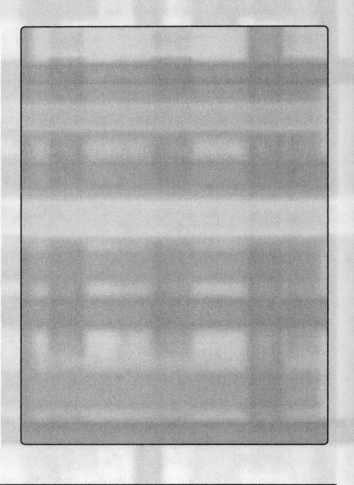

*Dear Lucky,*

*Lately, I've been trying to make friends outside my circle, but I'm really shy. What's the best way to approach others?*

*—Tongue Tied*

There are tons of ways to jumpstart a friendship. You don't have to get stressed or feel insecure. Clue in to what other girls are talking about in your already familiar, everyday environments. Who's into soccer? Who loves to read? You're bound to find other gals who share your interests. When you do, get in on the convo. You won't feel shy when you're talking about a subject that really interests you. Your gabbing skills will just come naturally. One chat won't result in a BFF, but it's a great beginning. You can do it!

It's time for you to show what an awesome friend you can be and make some true-blue buds. Your first step? Invite a girl from class (someone you seem to have a lot in common with) to do something fun with you. Do you skate? See if she wants to join you at the rink. Got assigned to work on a school project? Ask a girl if she wants to partner-up with you on it. Cool new movie just come out? Well, you get the picture! Also, try befriending another classmate who doesn't have a ton of friends or is on the shy side. Have her over after school one day— she'll probably really appreciate it! If it continues to be tough getting to know your classmates, plan to do something fun with a girl from your neighborhood or someone involved in one of your after-school activities. What—no after-school activities? Well, joining something fun outside of school is a great way to make new friends. As soon as you take an active role in getting to know others, it shouldn't be long before you have a bunch of new buds.

Spending the summer in a new town gives you a great chance to meet new buds. Does your dad live in a neighborhood with other kids around? Get outside and say "hello." Also, ask your dad if any of his friends have kids your age. Then, find out what's fun to do around town. Is there a community pool? Spend plenty of time there. A library? There might be a summer reading program for kids your age, so check it out. Don't get discouraged if you don't meet people right away. It might take some time and a little effort. If you really get the "I'm all alone" blues, reach out to your best buds back home through e-mail and phone calls (maybe your folks will get you a pre-paid calling card). Last, be sure to bring along a stack of good books for when you're just hanging out at home. Good luck!

# DO THE RIGHT THING

Can your friendships stand the test of time? They probably will if you know how to be a great pal! That means treating your BFFs well and being considerate about their feelings. It also means being true to yourself. Here are some ways you can avoid potential pal-dom pitfalls.

*Dear Lucky,*

*My BFF and I hang with different groups. Whenever I make plans with my group of friends, she asks why I don't want to hang with her. She's not the problem—it's the group of girls she spends time with. What should I tell her?*

*—Stuck in the Middle*

Honesty is the best policy. However, you can't just say, "I don't like hanging out with your group because your friends are the worst!" Explain to your BFF that you love spending time with her, but that having your own group of friends is really important to you. Not spending every waking moment together shouldn't damage your relationship. In fact, it could strengthen it. Spending 24/7 with *anyone* is bound to get stale every now and then, anyway. By scheduling quality one-on-one time, you two are more likely to really appreciate and enjoy each other's company. Plus, it's limiting to depend on one friend for your entire social life. This way, you have a wider social circle and more opportunities for fun! If being BFFs and sticking to your own circles works for you two, fab! Otherwise, is there any room for compromise? Do you like *any* of her friends? What about inviting her to get together with your crew this weekend? It's worth a go, don't you think?

**Dear Lucky,**

*I've been invited to two birthday parties on the same day and at the same time. One is for my BFF, and the other is for a friend from school. The school friend's party is going to be a blast, with a DJ, dancing, and boys! My BFF's party will be fun too, but all we are doing is going out to dinner and then a movie. I'd rather go to my other friend's party, but I don't want to let my BFF down. What should I do?*

*—In a Party Pickle*

I think you know what you should do. Your school friend's party might sound really cool, but it doesn't mean it will be better than your BFF's. For one, your BFF won't be there. I'm sure your school friend will understand your missing her party. But, would your BFF understand if you dissed her on her big day for another party? I don't think so. Maybe you and your best bud can stop by and make an appearance at your school friend's party after the movie. If your BFF says it's a no-go, accept it—her birthday only happens once a year!

**Dear Lucky,**

*I'm not sure why I care about this, but I'm upset because I saw my next-door neighbor's IM to my sister about whether or not to invite me to her birthday party. My neighbor is two years younger than I am, and we've always invited each other to our parties. We used to be friends, but now we're not as close as we once were. In the IM, she said she's worried that I might not have a good time because I'm older and wouldn't know anyone. I understand, but it hurts a bit—though I'm not even sure I'd go. What should I do?*

*—Feeling Left Out*

From the sound of it, it's not that your neighbor doesn't *want* you at her party—she's just worried you won't have a good time! Even though you played together as tots, now you're the cool, older girl, so she probably doesn't know if you'd even want to attend a party with younger kids. And like you said, you're not even sure you'd want to go. Since she's worried about your feelings, think about hers. Tell her you consider her a friend and would like to celebrate her birthday with her. If you don't feel comfortable doing the whole party thing, just drop by with a gift and split. What's important is showing her you still care about her.

*Dear Lucky,*

*I have three best friends. One of my BFF's dad lost his job, so now she can't afford to go out as often. The three of us planned on going to an ice show, but now she doesn't have the money to buy a ticket. I still want to go though. I feel sorry for her, but we can't stop doing things just because she has to, right?*

*—Totally Torn*

That's a tough one. You should feel bad for your friend's misfortune, but at the same time you can't pity her—because nobody likes that. Is there any way you and your friends can lend her the money to go? Or maybe offer to buy her a ticket as an early birthday or holiday present? If you can't afford to pay double admission, talk with your bud about you and your other two BFFs still going. Would she feel left out? Explain that you really want to go and have been looking forward to going for a while. She might not mind, especially once you acknowledge the situation and express sensitivity about it. But if you sense a little sadness, plan a fun sleepover for another night to make it up to her.

*Dear Lucky,*

*My BFF is going through a lot with her family. She's been really down and never wants to get together anymore. I'm worried about her. What should I do?*

*—Concerned Friend*

You can't fix her family's sitch, but what you *can* do is be there for her. Being constantly down and avoiding friends are signs that she probably needs help from a trusted adult. Recommend that she talk to a teacher, counselor, or caring relative. Meanwhile, show her *you* care by letting her talk when she needs to, and by suggesting fun activities you two can do together. Just keep reminding her about how much you value her friendship.

**Dear Lucky,**

*This girl invited me to a party, but we're hardly friends. I don't want to go, and I don't want to be her BFF. How do I let her down?*

**—Not Interested**

It's okay if you don't want to go to her party, but could you be jumping to conclusions by assuming she wants to be your BFF? You're not the *only* person invited! It's a party—you might have a good time, and maybe some of your friends will be there. If you go and end up having a terrible time, you're free to leave. Just come up with a nice excuse like, "Thank you for inviting me to your party. Unfortunately, I have to be home early, so my mom's picking me up." Give the girl a chance. Who knows? You might even wind up with a good friend.

## YOU SAID IT!

### FIVE RULES FOR FRIENDS

Boys are great, but sometimes they can interfere with even the strongest friendships. So before you let a boy come between you and your BFF, here are some rules to play by.

✿ *RULE ONE:* Don't get a crush on your BFF's boyfriend. There are zillions of boys out there, so try not to choose the one your friend likes.

✿ *RULE TWO:* Don't break plans with a girlfriend for a boy. It's hard on her when you want to hang out with a boy instead of your BFF all the time, and nothing makes it worse than when you cancel plans with her just so you can hang out with him. So stick with your original plans!

✿ *RULE THREE:* Try to get your friends to be buds with your boyfriend's friends. Friends can feel left out when you spend time with a BF, so why not ask your BF to involve his friends in plans so you can invite your friends along, too?

✿ *RULE FOUR:* Don't blab about your friends' crushes to your BF. Unless they want you to say something, you should keep their boy secrets under wraps. Just think how you'd feel if the whole school knew who you had a crush on!

✿ *RULE FIVE:* Make a promise not to let anything—or anyone—wreck your friendships. If your friendship is strong from the start, not even a boyfriend can break it. Remember—friendships can last forever but crushes rarely do.

—Chelsea, 14

# BOYS 'N' BUDS

At some point in every friendship, a boy is bound to get in the way. Trust me, I get a TON of questions about this issue. But you definitely don't have to choose between your friends and your crushes! Here are some ways to balance your buds and boys.

*Dear Lucky,*
*All my BFFs go out in a group with their crushes and don't ask me to join them because I don't have a BF. I feel hurt and left out. Should I say something?*

**—All Alone**

Talk to them about it. I doubt they exclude you on purpose. Chances are, your friends assume you won't want to hang with them and feel like a spare wheel. Explain that you don't resent them for having BFs but that you feel you're missing out on some fun. I'm pretty sure you'll be invited on their next outing once they understand that being in their group without a BF of your own is no biggie to you. And, come to think of it, why not ask if any of their BFs have a friend who could come along... who knows?

*Dear Lucky,*

*My friend likes the boy I used to like, but she's worried it will ruin our friendship if he likes her back. I'm so over him, and I really don't mind if they like each other. How can I make her understand it's okay?*

**—Over Him**

You and your bud seem genuinely concerned about each other's feelings. If you're really okay with her liking this boy, then tell her you appreciate her putting your friendship first but that you no longer like him like that. Give her your best—and mean it. No need to push the issue, though. Leave it to them to take it from there (or not).

**Dear Lucky,**

*My BFF said she didn't like this boy, and then I said that I liked him. Guess what she did? She said she liked him, too. That happens with her so often! Every time I like someone, she starts to like him, too. How can I tell her to get her own life?*

—**Crowded In**

I can see how it would be annoying to have someone constantly liking every boy you like, but I think your friend is probably just trying to be more like you—not trying to make you angry or steal all your crushes. Remind her that part of the reason you like having her as a friend so much is because of what is *unique* about her—and different from you.

**Dear Lucky,**

*My BFF likes this guy, and he likes her back. Now, she hangs out with him and all his friends more than with me and our friends. Help!*

—**Left Way Out**

I'll bet your friend isn't doing any of this on purpose. Let her know you've been feeling left out ever since she started hanging with this boy. Don't yell at her, blame her, or try to make her feel bad, because it will only cause her to feel guilty or angry. Instead, talk to her calmly. Explain that you understand why she wants to spend time with her new guy, but that you miss her and would love to spend some more quality time together. You might also suggest that you and your friends hang out with her crush and his friends. That could be fun!

**Dear Lucky,**

*My BFF likes this boy, but I don't think he likes her. That's not the problem though. This boy also flirts with me, and I really like him, too. What should I do?*

—**In a Bind**

Please don't let this boy get between you and your BFF. She obviously likes him. If he flirts with you, too, it's okay to be friendly back, but think twice before you get in the way of your friend's crush. A boy should never be a reason to end a friendship.

## YOU SAID IT!

### GETTING OVER A FRIEND'S CRUELTY

Getting over a friend's cruelty can be hard and takes a lot of time. It's been a year since I was friends with some girls who dumped me, and I'm just getting over the loss of my friends. The worst time is the period before you make new friends. Here are some tips to help you through it:

❀ *Talk to someone.* I waited too long to do that. You could talk with a parent, older sibling, a counselor, or another adult you trust. Just getting your feelings out makes you feel much better.

❀ *Write a letter to your friend.* Tell her how you feel. Make sure it's not a mean letter, just one that expresses your pain.

❀ *Writing in a journal helps.* You can put all your feelings down on paper, and no one else will ever have to read it.

❀ *And if all else fails? Punch a pillow.* Imagine that the pillow is the person who hurt you and take your feelings out on the pillow, not others!

—Rachel H., 14

---

*Dear Lucky,*

*My BFF just got a boyfriend. She always brags and tries to make me jealous because I don't have a BF. Without hurting her feelings, how can I let her know I don't want to hear it?*

*—Tired of Her Talk*

Most likely, she's not trying to hurt your feelings. She's probably excited about her crush and just wants to gab about him. If she continues to brag and it makes you uncomfortable, let her know. A real friend wouldn't want you to be jealous. Tell her you are confident about yourself and don't need a boyfriend to be happy. Then explain how her bragging affects you. If she is a good friend, she will appreciate your honesty and be more considerate of your feelings from now on.

**Dear Lucky,**

*I've been best friends with this girl since kindergarten. But she has a new BF, and I don't like him at all. He's around her all the time, even when she and I are hanging out. He really bothers me. Should I say something to her?*

*—Bugged by BFF's BF*

I understand how this boy can be a barrier. It used to be just you and your BFF hanging out all the time, right? All of a sudden, this boy is in the picture. Is it really that you don't like him—or is it that you don't like sharing her with him? Before you go bad-mouthing him to your bud, you need to figure out what's truly bugging you. Then, level with your friend about your feelings. If you feel you two don't get enough one-on-one time together, perhaps you can plan some girls-only fun. Remember, though, that she probably likes hanging out with and getting to know her new BF, so give her the time and space she needs right now. I'm sure your friendship will survive this BF and other BFs to come (including yours!).

# SAYING 'BYE TO YOUR BUDS

It's so sad when you or one of your good pals has to move away. Even if it's just a short distance, a move can take a toll on your relationship. Here are some tips to help you deal with the distance.

**Dear Lucky,**

*I'm going to a different school than my friends in the fall. I still want to be friends with them, but I'm scared they won't want to hang out with me anymore or that they might forget about me. What can I do?*

*—Sad to Split Up*

Splitting up is always a bummer, especially when it's you who's left out. If they are your true friends, they will still want to hang out—the only problem is finding the time. Seeing each other during the week could be hard, with homework and after-school activities, but you can still IM, e-mail, or call each other to chat. Also, plan to see each other on the weekends. It might be hard at first, but with a little extra effort, everything should work out fine.

Making new friends can definitely seem a bit intimidating to someone who's shy. But, no one says you have to jump into it full-force. Take it slow. See if any kids your age live in your new neighborhood. If so, work up the nerve to introduce yourself. School is also a great place to meet new friends. Chat it up with the girl who has a locker by yours. Or start a convo in gym class by asking a classmate to be your dribbling partner. Homeroom can also be a good place to meet new friends. Each time you work up the guts to talk to someone, you're one step closer to shaking your shyness—practice makes perfect.

## YOU SAID IT!

### I Miss You!

Are you moving? It's sad, I know. It happens to girls everywhere—and it happened to me. Here are some tips on dealing with it, staying close and, gulp, finding new friendships.

❀ *Hitting the new school year...without her.* You sit solo on the bus. The other kids all seem to have best friends already. And last night, you and your BFF held your "guess what I am wearing on the first day of school" talk over the phone. It's obvious what's missing here. But now that school is starting, you can meet a world of new people!

❀ *Where to begin?* Be the first person to say "hi" to kids at your school. Be polite, tell a girl about yourself, and ask her questions about herself. Just make sure that every other word out of your mouth is not about how great your old BFF and other old friends are.

❀ *Make new friends and keep the old.* You're back on your feet and feeling good. You have new friends, and things are going great. But don't get so caught up in your new social whirl that you forget your old friends. E-mail is a totally cheap, totally cool way to stay in touch. When you write, tell your old BFF and other friends what's up with you. And call if your parents say it's okay (long distance calls cost money, ya know). Send cute postcards of your new town. Little things mean a lot.

—April M., 14

It's hard when friends move, and you're right—things aren't the same. But you can still be BFFs. It just takes a little more effort! It's understandable that you want to visit her, but it's also understandable that your parents worry about letting you fly—and all by yourself (I assume). Can you come up with a compromise? Maybe your mom would be willing to travel with you. If your mom's not up for it, can your BFF visit you? Maybe her family is ready for a trip down Memory Lane! It will take planning, but the trick is to work something out that's agreeable to both families. Meantime, you guys can talk anytime you want! This isn't the Stone Age—you've got e-mail, IM, the phone, and, of course, good ol' snail mail! P.S. Keep in touch!

# CAN THIS FRIENDSHIP BE SAVED?

In a perfect world, you and your pals would never argue and you could always rely on your buds. Yeah, right! Every friendship has its ups and downs. At times, resolving conflict with pals can make friendships even stronger. Sometimes, though, you need to re-evaluate a relationship. Read on for how to deal when so-called friends do you wrong.

It's hard to trust a liar but, over time, friends can forgive one another and learn to trust again. Talk to your friend and ask her to explain why she lied to you. Make sure she understands just how much it hurt you and why you feel uneasy about trusting her anymore. Then remember that everyone makes mistakes. Think about your friendship and all the good times you two have had together. Realize how silly it would be to stay mad at her forever—as long as she doesn't make it a habit of being dishonest with you.

Whoa! What's up with that? While friendships vary from time to time in how close you feel toward each other, this seems extreme. While it's natural to get annoyed with a friend once in a while, saying that you hate someone's guts is severe and warrants some explaining…especially since you say you have no idea why this sudden icy shift started. At the very least, your friend should explain why she's saying such hurtful things. Maybe you did something to offend her or upset her that you don't even know about. E-mail her back and ask for an explanation, telling her that if you did something to hurt her, you'd like the chance to talk about it and try to work things out. After all, if she *was* your BFF, she should care enough about your friendship to at least give it a shot. Keep in mind, however, that even though you deserve an explanation, you might not get one. Maybe your friend is going through a weird phase or blaming you for something that's not your fault. You'll likely feel powerless and frustrated if that's the case, which is entirely understandable. Just remember that you did what you could to try to get the friendship back on track. Sometimes, that's all you can do.

Fighting with a friend feels awful, but bud battles are inevitable. Explain to your friend that refusing her letter didn't mean you wanted to give up on the friendship but that you weren't ready to deal right then. Tell her that your friendship is worth a lot to you and that you'd like to try to work things out. If she agrees to talk about it, you two should vow to break this pattern of ignoring each other and, instead, express your feelings openly and honestly. From now on, if you need some space, that's okay, but *say* it: "I need to get some distance to cool off before we discuss this."

## SIX SECRET STEPS TO GETTING OVER A BAD FRIEND

In fifth grade, I became best friends with a girl. Over the summer, I tried to get in touch with her but she never seemed to be home. The whole summer went that way. Right before school began again, I heard my so-called friend was saying horrible things about me! I felt terrible and betrayed. I'd poured out my soul to this person and there she was, gossiping about me. At school, we avoided each other. I was really sad about it for a long time, but slowly I was able to realize how to get over a bad friend. Here are six steps that really helped me:

1. True friends treat each other with consideration and thoughtfulness. Realize that if some girl is forgetting your friendship, she isn't a real friend.

2. If the person doesn't like or accept you the way you are, she isn't the type of friend you want anyway.

3. Don't let just one friend mean the world to you. Remember there are many people who care about you, so spend more time with them instead.

4. Do activities you love. Don't stop doing things that make you happy, and soon you'll feel better.

5. When your friends and family see you are hurt, their first reaction is to help you feel better. Let them cheer you up.

6. Remember—life will go on and, eventually, it won't hurt so much. No matter what it feels like now, time heals the pain.

—Andrea L., 13

### Dear Lucky,

*My best friend is a boy. I've gotten to know all of his friends and I like hanging out with them. But the girls in my class that I'm friends with give me a hard time. I love my guy friends, but I don't want to be totally alienated from the girls.*

—*Getting Grief*

My guess? Your girl friends probably just miss you (and perhaps they're a little jealous, too). Do your best to score some girls-only hang time. It's also a good idea to introduce your girl friends to your guy friends—maybe they will hit it off, and everyone can go out in a group. If you can't unite the two fronts, try to become a master of balance by spending hang time with both.

**Dear Lucky,**

*My BFF and I have been friends for seven years, but now she says another girl is her BFF. I'm really hurt and don't want to lose her.*

**—Losing a Friend**

If you two have been BFFs for seven years, I seriously doubt your friendship could go kaput just because there's another girl around. Do you still have as much fun with your friend? Do you continue to share the same interests and enjoy each other's company? Then, you two should be able to remain buds, even as you meet and become friends with other girls. Ever hear the saying, "Make new friends, but keep the old. One is silver, and the other gold"? It sounds like your friend has made a new "silver" friend, but let's hope she remembers who is "gold"!

**Dear Lucky,**

*My BFF and I have been fighting. She starts the fights but tells her mom everything is my fault. Now, her mom treats me differently.*

**—Unfairly Faulted**

Sounds like something's going on with your BFF, and she's taking it out on you. You've become her emotional punching bag, and that hurts! Is she struggling in school? Is she jealous of your good grades or a new crush? Is she feeling threatened because you usually click with her mom? Maybe she doesn't know how to appropriately express her emotions. And if something's upsetting her on the home front, she might be trying to get her mom's attention—even if it means dogging you. Perhaps, she's not even aware of what she's doing—or how it affects you. Regardless of her motives, you can't be too surprised when her mom runs a little cold around you. It's only natural for a mom to side with her daughter. That said, you might need a BFF break! Don't place blame—just suggest some time apart until the storm blows over. Hopefully, your BFF will realize you're trying to set things straight for a long and lasting friendship.

# KEEPING OLD FRIENDS WHILE MAKING NEW ONES

I made new friends and kept the old ones at the same time. At first, most of my new friends were not well-liked by my old friends, but now we're all great friends. Here's how I did it:

*STEP 1:* Don't be afraid to tell your old friends about your new friends. Just be sure to remind your old friends how important your friendship with them is to you and how much you like them.

*STEP 2:* Be willing to listen to what your old friends think about your new friends.

*STEP 3:* If your old friends think your new friends are cool, then you're set. But if your old friends disagree with letting new friends into your crew, follow the remaining steps.

*STEP 4:* Find out if there's anything the two sets of friends have in common, like sports or TV shows they like.

*STEP 5:* Once you find out, make sure they know they have something in common with each other.

*STEP 6:* They might want to all be friends—but then again, they might not. This is okay. But if they don't, follow the next steps.

*STEP 7:* Pick one of your old friends as your science lab or history report partner, and then ask if you can trade yourself for one of your new friends.

*STEP 8:* After you have paired them up, ask them how everything is going.

*STEP 9:* Be sure to spend equal time with them both.

*STEP 10:* Make sure your old friends hear about all the good things your new friends are doing and vice versa.

*STEP 11:* Here is the challenging part. Ask your old friends what problems are keeping you all from being on good terms. Armed with that, go back to your new friends and suggest some things they might change. Be sure to mention that your old friends will try to change, too.

*STEP 12:* Tell your old friends that you really, really want to let your new friends into the group. They don't have to be great friends as long as they are nice to each other. Then maybe they will become friends. That's what I did.

—Stacia B., 15

**Dear Lucky,**

*I think my BFF's dad doesn't like me. He never talks to me when I'm over at her house, and he never lets my BFF know when I call. What did I do wrong?*

—Hurt by Her 'Rent

I'm sure you haven't done anything wrong. He probably likes you just fine. Parents are busy, especially after long workdays, so it's a good idea not to take it too personally when they're not too friendly. Also, he could be stressed out about something that has nothing to do with you. That doesn't mean he dislikes you—it just means he might be tired and want some time to relax. But, if he's *always* short with you, maybe he's just not a warm and fuzzy guy. All you can do is be yourself and always be courteous when you're visiting your BFF. Always say "thank you" after your visit and even try to start up a convo with him if you want. It might show him how hard you are trying to earn his respect.

## YOU SAID IT!

### DEALING WITH PEER PRESSURE

Ugh, peer pressure. I hate whoever invented it. It's so hard to deal with it sometimes I could scream. But, believe me, it feels good to avoid peer pressure because doing things that are bad won't get you anywhere except in trouble. The following tactics always work for me:

*SITUATION ONE:*
Friends are making fun of a girl behind her back.
*SOLUTION:* Try changing the subject. If that doesn't work, walk away. Not rudely—act like it's just out of boredom or that you've got other things to do.

*SITUATION TWO:*
Your friends are thinking about shoplifting at the candy store.
*SOLUTION:* Complain of a stomachache, hunch over, and hobble out of the store. A little lame, I know, since you should be setting them straight—but this will keep you out of trouble and your conscience clear.

*SITUATION THREE:*
A boy likes you, but he's not exactly your Prince Charming.
*SOLUTION:* Remember other people have feelings, too. And if you reject this boy, other boys might be afraid to approach you in the future. Try this: "I think you are one of the nicest people I know (it's okay to lay it on a little thick), but I really don't like you like that. It's cool, though, if we hang out and do things as friends." Then follow through, and bring a friend with you whenever you hang out with him.

—Maya, 14

# BONUS QUIZ:
## ARE YOU A GOOD FRIEND?

*Find out if you tiptoe around your friends' feelings or tell 'em like it is.*
*—Kristen R., 13*

**1. Your best friend tries to pair you up with her dorky cousin for couples-skate at the rink. You:**

    a. look at her disgustedly and say, "I'm not skating with that creep!"

    b. say, "Sure, but just this once."

    c. skate away and pretend you didn't hear her.

**2. Your crush asks you to watch a video with him the same night you and your best friend had already planned to see a movie together. You:**

    a. ditch your bud and go to watch a vid with your crush.

    b. ask your friend if it's okay for you to invite Romeo to meet you guys at the theater.

    c. take your cordless off the hook that night and tell both of them the next day that you forgot that your grandparents were visiting from Finland.

**3. Your friend wants you to go to the arcade, but your parents said you're not allowed to waste money on games. You:**

    a. say, "Where did you come up with an idea like that?"

    b. say, "Yes, but can you lend me some money?"

    c. tell her, "Maybe some other time."

**4. Your friend asks if you want to make prank phone calls after school. She says if you don't, she will spread rumors about you. You:**

    a. threaten to dump her as a friend if she doesn't stop pressuring you.

    b. politely say, "No, I'd rather not," and walk away.

    c. look at her and say, "Huh? Did you say something?"

**5. Your boyfriend doesn't like your best friend because he thinks she's a troublemaker. Lately, you're starting to see what he's saying. You:**

    a. tell your best friend you are never speaking to her again.

    b. nicely confront your friend about your worries.

    c. tell your boyfriend you are too busy thinking about a test to worry about anything else.

**6. You have a fair-weather friend. One second, she is like your shadow. The next, she acts like she hates you. You:**

    a. totally blow up at her for treating you this way.

    b. tell her the sitch: "You treat me with respect all the time, or you get nada from me."

    c. ignore her. She'll get the message after a while.

**7. A friend's little bro and sis insist on coming along every time you and your friend go out together. You are getting annoyed. You:**

    a. angrily confront your best friend about her bratty sibs.

    b. tell her you would like it if the two of you could spend some time alone occasionally.

    c. steer clear of the group outings until your friend gets the clue.

**8. Your best friend is moving 3,000 miles away, thanks to her parents. However, she invites you to a going-away party. You:**

    a. yell at your friend and never call or write her at her new home.

    b. go to the party and try to have fun—it might be the last time you ever see her.

    c. pretend you didn't get her invitation and blow off the party.

**9. Your BFF really hits it off with your latest crush! You're steaming. You:**

    a. blow up at her for liking him, and keep him as far from her as possible.

    b. stay calm when she goes to the mall with him—and pray they don't have fun.

    c. tell her she should ignore your crush's total cuteness, and hope she finds a new guy.

**10. You just got this totally cool new bike for your birthday, and your friend wants to try it out. You:**

    a. hide your bike in the garage whenever she is around.

    b. tell her she can ride it for a day as long as she takes care of it.

    c. ignore her and show off your bike to everyone, making her totally jealous.

**11. She did it again—your friend lied to you. You're getting tired of it. You:**

    a. tell some lies to her, and then see how she likes being treated that way.

    b. confront her nicely about her lying to you, and wait for her response.

    c. ignore the lies, and change the subject whenever she tries to bluff you.

# SCORING

### Mostly A's: Face-it Friend!
You like to get back at your friend with either actions or words. And you like to voice your opinion, but sometimes you don't do it very tactfully. Why not? It won't get you anywhere. Give her a chance. Ask her questions, and nicely resolve any situations that arise.

### Mostly B's: In Between Bud
You are a great friend! You like to consider your buds' feelings. But be careful. In some situations, sensitivity is good. However, you need to be sure you're not being walked on!

### Mostly C's: Pretending Pal
You like to ignore your problems. Uh-oh! Not a good sitch to be in, girl friend. You have to tell your friends how you're feeling. You can't just hide in that little hole forever.

# CHAPTER 2

# ON THE HOME FRONT

**N**o matter what, your family bonds are likely to be stronger than any other relationships in your life. Even though you might not get along with everyone in your family all the time (who does?!), deep down you know they'll be there for you through thick and thin.

Just that knowledge alone can make dealing with family issues much easier. But in case you need a little extra input, here are some ideas for handling everything from parental sitches to sibling snafus.

# OH, BROTHER...OH, SISTER!

Most sibs get along great sometimes; other times, they argue. There are moments when getting along with your sibs seems impossible! (Trust me—I know.) Does your little brother pester you? Is your big sis ignoring you? Read on!

*Dear Lucky,*

*I'm the youngest of five girls, and my sisters think I'm a little brat or something. Even my mom and dad treat me like a baby. How can I get my family to see that I'm not in diapers anymore?*

*—Not a Baby Anymore*

I know what you're talking about! It's totally frustrating when people—especially family—treat you like a baby. Book some alone time with the 'rents to let them know you're ready to be taken more seriously. If you give them specific examples of how mature you are—like how you always clear the dinner table and get your homework done without being told—maybe they'll realize you're ready for more responsibility and independence. Also, talk to them about how they treat you in front of your sibs. If your parents ease up on the babying, maybe your sibs will see you differently, too. And remember that actions speak louder than words. So, after explaining you want more respect, behave like you deserve it. For instance, when conflicts with your sisters come up, work them out yourself. Don't go running to your parents—like a baby.

*Dear Lucky,*

*I fight with my little sister because she constantly comes into my room without knocking and snoops through my stuff when I'm not home. How can I make her stop?*

*—Feeling Invaded*

Little sisters can be annoying. But probably the reason she hangs around is because she looks up to you. Even if she acts bratty, she's likely just trying to get your attention. She wants to hang out with you, and maybe this is the only way she knows to get you to notice her. Explain that you love her but that you also need your privacy. Set up some specific guidelines, like your room is off limits when you aren't there, and she must knock before entering when you are. Instead of squabbling, make an effort to spend a little bonding time with your sib.

*Dear Lucky,*

*My brother and sister are really popular and good-looking, but I'm not. They've had tons of girlfriends (my brother) and boyfriends (my sister), and I've never had one. I'm not shy or anything, but boys don't seem to like me. How do I become more popular like my sibs?*

*—Feeling Forgotten*

Do you really want a boyfriend, or do you just want to keep up with your brother and sister? While your sibs are probably really cool, you also have qualities you should be proud of. So concentrate on all that good stuff, and get to know more people around you. Start conversations with kids you haven't gotten a chance to know, and join clubs to meet others with similar interests. Having a group of for-real friends is what "popularity" is really all about, anyway.

## YOU SAID IT!

### HOW I DEALT WITH MY SNOOPY LITTLE SISTER

My little sister always used to go through my things. She would go in my room when I wasn't there, borrow clothes without asking me, and take stuff that wasn't hers. I told my mom about it, and my sister got in trouble for it—but she still kept snooping! Finally, I figured out a few ways to keep her out of my business for good:

1. Lock your door! My mom let me put a latch on my door so I can lock my room when I'm out. (If your parents won't let you do that or you share a room with your sister, this probably won't work.)

2. If you write in a journal or diary, get one that locks and keep the key with you at all times.

3. Let your sister know which clothes of yours she can wear. Keep your favorite stuff off limits, but let her wear *some* things.

4. Let her hang out with you more. I think my sister snooped because she wanted to be involved in my life. The more I let her do stuff with me, the less she snooped!

—Kara H., 15

*Dear Lucky,*

*My sister is in ninth grade and plays varsity soccer. She also runs track and has broken four school records—and this is only her fourth meet ever! I like sports and all, but I get really upset when I'm compared to her. She practices soccer three hours a day and usually runs four miles afterward. I'm expected to do all that now, too. My sister is really nice to me, but all our coaches think I can be just as good as she is—they push me way too hard. How can I get everyone to stop making comparisons?*

*—Unfairly Compared*

Don't torture yourself. I'm sure you have plenty of talents and goals of your own. Find something you like doing. Do some exploring to figure out your interests. This way, you'll have the freedom to be your own star. Instead of worrying about being a record-breaker, just enjoy the process of discovering more about yourself. As for your sister and soccer coaches, let them know you love the team and will happily cheer them on—from the stands!

*Dear Lucky,*

*I'm an identical twin, and people always confuse me with my sister. We have done everything to look different, from changing our clothes to our haircuts. What else is left for us to do?*

*—Double Trouble*

It seems like you have made every effort to be seen as individuals. You probably have distinct personalities, too, no matter how similar you look on the outside. I'm sure your close friends and family can tell you two apart, right? So who cares what everyone else thinks? If they can't tell you two apart, then they're not taking the time to get to know you well enough. Accept the fact that you have a sister who looks like you, and don't dwell on it. There will always be a teacher or relative who gets mixed up. (I have an Aunt Edna who insists on calling me by my little bro's name—now, *that's* bad.) And, admit it—isn't it great to be a twin? I've always wished I had one!

# "THEY TREAT ME LIKE I AM TWO!"

Do you ever feel as though your parents still think of you as a tyke? Sometimes, I feel like my parents will think of me as their little girl when I'm 30! But I've certainly discovered some ways to earn the trust of parents. Here are some tips for getting the big-girl recognition you deserve.

*Dear Lucky,*

*My parents are way overprotective! I'm not allowed to have a boyfriend, and I feel guilty because I've been talking to this boy. How can I tell my parents in a way that won't make them totally freak out?*

*—Feeling Sheltered*

Figure out a good time to talk with your parents—like on a leisurely Saturday, not on a busy week night or right after they get home from work. Tell them you're ready for more freedom. Remind them you're responsible—you're always home by curfew, and you stay on top of your schoolwork. (Um…you *do*, right? If not, shape up!) Explain that there's a boy you like and that you don't want to keep it a secret from them. If they aren't sold, remember that they're just looking out for you. It's tough for some parents to watch their kids grow up, so try to understand where they're coming from. Why not invite this boy over to meet them? Be patient, stay calm, and, hopefully, your parents will accept your crush.

## How I Got My Parents to Trust Me

If your parents don't trust you, show them how responsible you are! Here are some ways to do it:

❀ *Tell them what's up.* Be sure to keep them informed of what's going on in your life so they don't feel as though you're hiding stuff from them.

❀ *Follow their rules.* If you have a curfew, stick to it. And if they ask you to do something, do it.

❀ *Ask for their advice.* You might not want to follow everything they say but, believe it or not, your parents have some good tips. After all, they were young once.

❀ *Be accountable.* If you do something wrong, own up to it. Accepting blame shows that you can handle the consequences of your actions.

❀ *Know when to stop pushing for something.* If your parents say "no" even after you plead your case, you have to accept it. They're your parents, and they have the final word. But once they know you can be trusted, chances are they'll give you more freedom and privileges.

—Laurel W., 13

*Dear Lucky,*
*My BFF is having a huge bash. I'm allowed to go, but my mom wants me home by 8:30 p.m.! How can I convince her to let me stay out later just this one time?*
       *—Needing a New Curfew*

Hit Mom up for a special exception. Tell her you appreciate that she's letting you go but that you really want to stay until the party is over—with her approval, of course. Remind Mom you are a responsible gal (usually, staying out later is a responsibility issue). Finish your homework, pick up your room, load the dishwasher. Hopefully, your mom will notice how dependable you are and might be willing to give you some leeway. Be sure she has your pal's phone number so she can call the parental hosts. If keeping in touch is an issue, tell her you'll call her at 8:30 to let her know you're okay and then call her again when the party's over to let her know you're ready to head home. Also, be sure how and with whom you're getting home is spelled out in advance. If you're mature and reasonable about your approach, your mom might bend the rules this time. If not, make the best of the time you've got!

**Dear Lucky,**

*My mom doesn't give me any freedom! She acts like I'm still in first grade. She never lets me go to the mall or movies with my friends unless there's an adult going along. I'm almost 12. How long do I have to wait until she trusts me?*

**—Needing My Freedom**

It's hard for moms to stop babying their kids. In her eyes, you're still her little girl. All moms are like this to some degree. Talk to your mom. Tell her you love her and appreciate how much she cares about you but that you think you're old enough to start doing things on your own. Ask her to give you a test run so you can prove to her that you're ready to be more independent. Ask her if you can go to the movies with your friends, without her. If everything goes well and you keep to the plan, she should see that you're old enough to do some things without a chaperone. Remember to take baby steps on your path to independence!

**Dear Lucky,**

*My mom always checks my e-mails. She even deletes some of my messages without telling me. I haven't done anything to make her distrust me. What can I do about it?*

**—No Privacy**

Tell your mom you feel she's totally invading your privacy. Talk to her in a mature and calm manner, and ask why she's reading and deleting your e-mail. Find out if there is a reason she distrusts you. I'm guessing it's not *you* she doesn't trust. She, like most parents, is probably concerned about the scary things that sometimes happen when kids chat with the wrong people on the Internet. If this is the case, assure her that if you ever come across any suspicious or unsavory e-mail, you will let her know immediately so she can screen it. Hopefully, she'll understand where you're coming from and will stop snooping. If she continues, you can always switch to snail mail (I know, I know).

*Dear Lucky,*

*My dad has given me more responsibilities than my 15-year-old sister, and I'm only 11! It's more than I can handle! He won't listen when I try to tell him. What should I do?*

*—On Chore Overload*

Your dad is probably giving you so many responsibilities because he believes you're capable of handling them, not because he's trying to be mean or favor your older sister. By giving you responsibilities, your dad is showing that he thinks you're organized and on top of your game, but even parents can sometimes miscalculate a situation. While taking on responsibilities is part of getting older and demonstrates your maturity and dependability, you shouldn't feel overloaded. Since you've already tried to talk with him, why not write a letter? Explain that you're not trying to ditch your chores but that you feel overwhelmed with everything you have to do. Ask if you can work together to make a list of responsibilities you feel comfortable taking on and cut out some that aren't as important to your dad. That way, your dad will know you just want enough time to do everything right without getting stressed out.

# FAMILY FRICTION

Dealing with family issues isn't always easy. Disagreements are part of life, and it's unrealistic to think life with your 'rents, your sibs, and other family members will always be blissful. Here's how to combat trouble on the home front.

*Dear Lucky,*

*My mom won't let me wear any makeup, not even lip gloss. It's not like I would cake it on. What do I do?*

*—Ready for Cosmetics*

Talk to your mom about why you feel ready to wear makeup. Suggest that you start with lip gloss and maybe a little mascara, which won't make you look much older (that's probably why your mom has a problem with it). Be cool and calm. Don't yell or whine. After you lay out your suggestions, the ball is in her court. Remember, ultimately the decision is hers. So if the answer is still "no," take it like a pro. Listen to her reasons, and thank her for hearing you out.

### TEN WAYS TO MAKE YOUR PARENTS PROUD

Do you really want to make your folks happy? It's not so hard.
Here are ten things you can do that will make your parents' day.

1. Surprise them by setting the dinner table without being asked.

2. Get your homework done before they ask about it.

3. If your mom has had a really busy day, offer to do an extra chore for her.

4. Spend a Friday night hanging out with them.

5. Volunteer to watch your younger sister or brother upstairs while they watch a movie in peace downstairs.

6. Get up extra early and make them breakfast in bed.

7. Make your bed, and then make theirs, too.

8. Help them figure out their new computer.

9. Thank your mom for making such a great dinner—even if it didn't taste so great.

10. Tell them you love them!

—Hayley G., 13

*Dear Lucky,*

*Every year, my aunt has a summer barbecue reunion thing. But this year, my BFF's family is having a party the same day. I really want to go to my friend's party. How do I let my family down without hurting their feelings?*

*—Party Pooper*

I totally get why you want to hit your BFF's bash, but your aunt's party sounds like a family tradition. Spending time with the fam is priority numero uno. But don't get bummed just yet. Could you bail a bit early from your aunt's and show up fashionably late to your friend's shindig? As long as you let everyone know how much it means to you to be able to attend both, your family might let you skate out a bit early.

*Dear Lucky,*

*My parents smoke, and it bothers me. I stink like smoke, and it grosses me out. Whenever I talk to them about it, they say they're trying to quit. What can I do?*

**—Smoked Out**

Ask them—nicely—if they'll restrict smoking to one part of the house or, better yet, outside. Tell them you hate smelling like an ashtray and would rather not inhale smoke. Do they know secondhand smoke is a huge cause of sickness—and can lead to cancer and other smoking-related diseases? For important info, run a search on the Internet. Maybe your encouragement will help them quit or at least get them thinking about it on a whole new level (especially when they're smoking every cig while standing under a vent or outdoors in bathrobes on rainy nights).

*Dear Lucky,*

*My parents never say, "I love you." We're just not a huggy family, but when I hear my friends say, "I love you, too," on the phone to their parents, it makes me sad.*

**—Needing More**

All families are different. Just because your family isn't particularly affectionate doesn't mean your parents don't love you! They *do* love you—more than you probably know. But, it's understandable if you're sad. Everybody likes to be reminded they're loved—especially by parents. Likely, your parents were raised in homes where love wasn't verbalized, so they're not used to saying, "I love you." But surely they show you they love you in other ways, right? After a bad day, does Mom whip up your favorite spaghetti-and-meatballs dinner? When was the last time your dad missed one of your soccer games? Almost everything they do, they do *because* they love you—even if they don't say it. But, unless you say something, they'll never know how you feel. And, hey, why not set the example yourself. Your actions can create change. Say, "I love you," to your parents before going to bed, or hug your mom when you get home from school. See if that helps them to reciprocate.

*Dear Lucky,*

*My grandma is so old-fashioned. I have a new spaghetti-strap dress I want to wear to a family wedding. My mom doesn't object, but my grandma says it's inappropriate and it offends her. Should I ignore my grandmother or what?*

*—Dressing Dilemma*

Grandparents are great, but they can sometimes be a little behind the times. You don't want to hurt your grandma's feelings, though, so talk to her instead of ignoring her. Let her know your mom approves of your style. Go for a compromise—like wear the dress with a wrap or a little cardigan. If your grandma won't budge, consider saving the dress for another occasion when it will be appreciated (or at least when it won't cause offense)!

## YOU SAID IT!

### DEALING WITH DIVORCE

When my parents got divorced, it was really hard on me. They fought a lot, and my mom didn't want me to spend any time with my dad. Things are finally better, but maybe what I learned can help you. If your parents are getting a divorce, keep these things in mind:

❀ *Remember that it's not your fault.* What's happening with your parents is not about you—it's about them, so don't ever feel responsible for causing their unhappiness.

❀ *Try to spend time with both parents.* Even if you wind up living with just one parent most of the time, be sure to spend time with the other parent, too. If one parent doesn't understand or doesn't want you to be around the other parent, explain that it's important for you to have a relationship with both of them and that you aren't taking sides by wanting to spend time with the other parent.

❀ *Talk to a friend or an adult when things get bad.* My best friend was there for me, and I could always talk to her about what was going on. That helped a lot.

❀ *Remember that it gets easier with time.* You'll adjust to things as time goes by, so don't think it's always going to be as bad as it may seem now!

—Marissa A., 14

# THE BIG D

Divorce isn't just hard on parents; it's hard on kids, too. And just when you think you have the whole divorce thing worked out, step-parents enter to make life even more challenging! Here are some ways you can cope with today's changing families.

*Dear Lucky,*

*My folks are divorced, and my mom has custody of me. But my dad always asks if I'll live with him when I'm older. If I do, I'll have to change schools and leave my friends. Plus, I'll miss my mom. But I'm afraid to hurt my dad's feelings. What can I do?*

*—Dad's Daughter, Too*

I totally understand that you don't want to give up your friends and familiar surroundings. If you're happy where you are, tell your dad. Not living with him doesn't mean you don't love him, and it doesn't even mean you don't want to live with him—it just means you're doing what's best for yourself. Explain how much you love your school and friends. Tell him you love him, too, and that you're psyched he wants you to live with him but that you'd rather stay with things as they are. Suggest more time together, like going out during the week instead of just on weekends. Maybe you two could take a trip. What about living with him for the summer? You might even discover your dad lives in a pretty cool place and has a bunch of fun neighbors. But you should never feel like you have to do something you're not comfy doing just to make someone else happy—even if that someone is dear old Dad. He wants his girl to be happy and, if that means staying with your mom, he ought to understand.

**Dear Lucky,**

*I just found out my parents want to get a divorce, but they're waiting until after I graduate from high school. I don't know if I can live with them fighting and being unhappy any longer. How do I deal with this?*

*—Feeling the Friction*

Kids should never be made to feel like they are in the middle of their parents' marital problems. You need to tell them how you feel. Let them know it's unbearable for you to think that they could be happier apart but instead insist on staying together for your sake. It's not healthy for anyone to live around constant fighting. Since this is a delicate, serious situation, you might ask that you and your parents have this conversation with a family therapist present, to act as a mediator while the three of you discuss things.

**Dear Lucky,**

*I always thought I had the perfect family, but I think my parents want a divorce. They fight, and they don't even seem to love each other anymore. All my friends have divorced parents, and they hate it. They have to go to counselors and don't get to pick which parent they live with. I don't want to be one of those girls. Help!*

*—Frightened*

It's frightening to think about your parents divorcing, but no family is perfect. When any family goes through a change, it's difficult for everyone involved. But understand that this change could actually improve your family situation. If your parents fight a lot, they might be happier apart. Also, just because your friends have had bad experiences doesn't mean you have to be "one of those girls." Talk honestly with your parents about your fears, and ask them to be open with you. This way, if they *do* divorce, you'll be better prepared. Remember that you can still have close relationships with both parents even, if they are no longer married.

*Dear Lucky,*

*I feel guilty about this but, lately, I wish my mom hadn't married my step-dad. I feel like he steals her from me. Around him, she's stricter—not like a friend. I don't want to tell her because, one day, I'll leave and won't want my mom to be alone.*

*—Feeling Jealous*

Incorporating step-parents into your life is an adjustment. It's perfectly natural to resent sharing your mom, but try not to think of it as a competition. After all, no matter how much time they spend together, your step-dad can never really steal your mom away—you're her daughter and nothing changes that! Reassure your mom that you're glad she's happy, but explain (without whining) that you feel she treats you differently—harsher—around your step-dad. Tell her you understand the discipline thing but that you miss spending time with her. She ought to be impressed with your honesty and maturity!

*Dear Lucky,*

*My parents are divorced, and I have to take turns spending holidays with them. I hate it. My mom's remarried, and sometimes I'm supposed to go with her and my step-dad. But then I feel bad for my dad. How can I be sure he doesn't have lonely holidays?*

*—Bounced Around*

Holidays can be tricky for kids with divorced parents. But you do have options. If your parents are on good terms, ask your mom if it's okay to invite your dad to an occasional holiday dinner. If not, offer to divide your time. Maybe you could have one holiday dinner with your mom, for example, and spend the next day with your dad, or vice versa? Or, what if you spend the morning of a holiday with your mom and have dinner with your dad? What you're shooting for is compromise so you can spend cool celebratory time with both 'rents.

# BONUS QUIZ:
## ARE YOU RESPONSIBLE?

*Do you give your parents good
reason to trust you? Take this quiz to find out.*

—Katie F., 12

**1. You're in line for a smoothie at the mall's food court, when you realize it's twenty minutes past curfew. Uh-oh. You:**

a. call your parents, let them know you're running late, and apologize profusely for losing track of the time.

b. race home and hope the folks are fast asleep.

c. come up with a doozy of a story for why you're so late.

**2. Your mom says PG-13 movies are off limits. But when you get to the theater, your buds have already bought tickets to the new Adam Sandler flick, rated PG-13. You:**

a. bow out and tell them you'll meet them after the movie.

b. see the movie, and avoid the subject when your folks ask how the movie was.

c. tell your parents about the movie—but lie and say it was rated PG.

**3. Your mom doesn't want you wearing makeup to school, so you:**

a. go natural and hope she'll change her mind soon!

b. wear tinted lip gloss only—after all, that's not *really* makeup.

c. paint your face up once you get to school, and wash it all off before you go home.

**4. Your brother gets in a minor fender-bender in your mom's car and he asks you not to tell. You:**

a. promise him you won't say a word...as long as he tells them first!

b. keep quiet unless your parents confront you about the dent in the car.

c. ask your bro how much your silence is worth to him and negotiate a deal.

**5. The rule at your house is no Internet after 9 p.m. But you're dying to see if your crush sent you an e-mail, so you:**

a. ask your parents for an exception to the rule just this once.

b. call your friend and have her log on to your account to check things out.

c. make sure the folks drop off to sleep before you do a quick e-mail check.

**6. You told the people you baby-sit for that you would sit Saturday night, but your friend has just invited you to her place that night for popcorn and to watch a DVD. You:**

a. thank your friend for the invite but explain that you already have made a commitment and are sticking with it.

b. ask the family's other sitter to substitute for you on Saturday, and explain to them that you've got the whole thing covered.

c. call early Saturday and tell the people you sit for that you're sick and can't baby-sit that night.

# SCORING

***Mostly A's: Dependable Daughter***
You are super responsible and trustworthy! Your parents know you'll tell the truth and accept responsibility for your actions, so they're likely to reward you with even more privileges.

***Mostly B's: Tricky 'Tween***
While you don't outright break the rules, you find clever ways to get around them. One of these days, your parents will catch on. And you know what? They'll only get stricter with you when that happens.

***Mostly C's: Bender and Breaker***
How do you deal with all your parents' rules? Simple—you just break 'em. But if you keep this up, your parents could lose all trust in you. Being responsible and honest shows maturity so, next time you're faced with a decision, do the right thing!

# CHAPTER 3

# SCHOOL SOLUTIONS

**S**chool should be an awesome experience (okay, minus all those pop quizzes and grueling tests)! Why, you ask? Well, you are not only there to learn, but also to develop your social skills. School is, after all, probably where you meet most of your gal pals and crushes. What's more, you get the opportunity to learn about new things and hone your talents through all those electives and extra-curriculars.

# BE A SCHOOL STAR

Between friends, sports, and clubs, it's easy to forget you're also at school to get an education! Check out these A+ tips on making the grade and making the most of your school days.

**Dear Lucky,**

No matter how hard I try, I don't do well on tests. I panic! What should I do?

—Test Troubles

Tests can make anyone nervous (that's normal), but the more prepared you are, the less likely you'll have a major panic attack. So, think about the last time you had trouble with a test. Was it because you hadn't studied or didn't know the subject matter well enough? If that's the case, then be as ready as you can be by studying hard. If you're having a tough time understanding things, get a tutor or ask your teacher to help you out. If you still get worked up, even when you're ultra-prepared, relax yourself before the test. Take a few deep breaths, and think positive thoughts. Hope you ace your next exam!

**Dear Lucky,**

I will be switching schools soon. I'm afraid I will forget everything and make a total goof of myself. My biggest fear is that I'll forget my locker combination. Do you have any advice?

—Too Tense

Relax. Everything will be fine. Starting a new school is definitely a big deal, but you aren't alone. An entire class of kids will be going through the same thing. If you're worried about forgetting things, buy a planner. Write down everything—class schedule, locker combination, bus schedule, etc. As the year goes on, you'll commit these things to memory but, at first, refer to your planner whenever you draw a blank. Also, make new friends—there's safety in numbers. Get involved in an activity or two after school. You'll meet people you have lots in common with. Lost? Don't know where you're going? Never be afraid to ask for help. Find a teacher or school administrator (or a super-cute boy) to help you find your way.

**Dear Lucky,**

*I dread school because my mom and I fight a lot about my grades. To be honest, I haven't been doing all that well. I work really hard, but she doesn't believe it! I want to be a doctor when I grow up. But, my mom always reminds me how hard I'll have to work to become a doctor and that I really need to "buckle down now!" How can I get her to realize I am working hard without her blowing up?*

*—Overwhelmed*

Show your mom how hard you're working by letting her see what you're doing. Show her your homework before you start it, and then sit down at a place where she can see you—like the kitchen table or something—to get it done. When you finish, share your completed work with her and explain what you did. Make this a routine. If you need help with anything, ask your mom to give you a hand so she sees you're trying to improve. Getting extra help from teachers is also a great idea. It shows you're genuinely interested in learning and upping those grades. Your mom and teachers should be impressed—and, hopefully, those fights will be fewer.

**Dear Lucky,**

*My BFF cheats off me in science class, and my teacher never notices. I can't ask her to stop because she'll get mad at me. What can I do?*

*—Cheater's Friend*

Stand up for yourself. Explain to your BFF that you're not comfortable with her cheating. Also, mention that you don't want someone else taking credit for your work (not to mention, what if your answers are wrong?) and that it's completely against the rules and could get you *both* in trouble. Then, offer to help her study for the next test. That's what friends are for, right?

# IT'S ALL ABOUT EXTRA-CURRICULARS

The best way to make your days at school super-enriching is to get involved in activities outside of academics. You know—things like sports, fun clubs, and organizations that interest you. Need some ideas? Keep reading!

*Dear Lucky,*

*I just made varsity basketball, and I'm the youngest person on the team. I don't know the other girls, and they treat me like I'm invisible. They don't talk to me, and I never have a partner for drills. I usually dribble with the coach. It really hurts my feelings. What can I do?*

*—Alone on the Court*

Congrats on making varsity! Too bad the other girls are dampening your achievement, though. But it doesn't have to be that way. Over time, as you practice and play together more, you'll get to know the other players better and feel more involved in the team dynamics, and, hopefully, they'll come to see you as their teammate. For now, make small talk in the locker room or ask someone to be your drill partner. While it might seem hard at first, being friendly can go a long way. If things don't change, talk to your coach. Maybe she can assign partners for drills or let the team captain know you feel left out.

*Dear Lucky,*

*I want to perform in the school play, but people say I'm not popular enough to do so. What's up?*

*—Drama Girl*

You're getting some bogus advice! Performing isn't a popularity contest—it's about talent. And the only way you'll be able to develop your talent is by giving it a try. So sign up for drama class, and polish up your acting skills. No doubt, getting involved in theater will also give you the boost of confidence you need to ignore comments like, "You're not popular enough," and keep you from letting others deter you from doing what you want to do. You've got to believe in yourself or no one else will!

## YOU SAID IT!

## MY TOP 10 TIPS FOR SCHOOL SURVIVAL

These ideas help me stay organized, friendly, and active during the school year.

**10.** *Make a schedule for yourself.* And stick to that schedule.

**9.** *If you find that you are getting lazy or your grades are dropping, talk to your teacher and/or parents.* Maybe they'll have suggestions that'll be helpful.

**8.** *Don't sign up for too many extracurricular activities.* You'll find yourself overloaded with stuff to do.

**7.** *Take part in class by answering questions.* Don't be one of those people who don't answer questions—you'll learn a lot less if you just sit there.

**6.** *Don't rely on everybody else or everything will come falling on top of you.* Take responsibility for your own work.

**5.** *Always make friends when you can.* Friends make school easier—and it can never hurt to have one more!

**4.** *If someone is mean, stand up for yourself and for your buds.* If that person doesn't stop being a jerk, talk to an adult who can help you out.

**3.** *Respect your teachers.* Even though some of your teachers may be a total snore, you need her and those good grades to pass the class.

**2.** *Your work should come before play.* If you don't sit down until 8 p.m. to do your homework, you might get tired and get bad grades.

And the **No. 1** tip to remember during the school year is this:

**1.** *Have fun, and always be yourself!*

—Lindsay G., 14

**Dear Lucky,**

*I want to run for a school office, but I'm not that popular. Should I even try?*

*—Ready to Run*

Absolutely! After all, what better way to get to know other students and let them get to know you than by being involved? Ask the teacher in charge of the elections for advice on getting your name out there. Then, have a few friends help with your campaign, and get going! Make colorful signs with catchy slogans (rhyming ones are always good), or come up with things like buttons or handmade T-shirts with your campaign slogan on them. If there's a forum for speeches or a debate with other candidates, work hard on your points and rehearse what you're going to say. Even if you don't win, it'll be a fun experience and your name will be out there. Then next time you run, you'll be well-known!

**Dear Lucky,**

*I just started at a brand new school, and I feel bored and lonely. How can I have a better time at school?*

*—Need a Life*

There are surely a bunch of clubs, organizations, or activities your school offers that you would enjoy! Ask a teacher or another student, or check out your school's bulletin boards or newsletters for opportunities. Can't think of any interests or hobbies? Dive into something new and different. That's the only way to know whether you'll like a new activity or not.

**Dear Lucky,**

*My friends and I have a club we originally called "The Friendship Club." But we hated the name and came up with a new one everybody likes except for one girl. I told her she should just leave the club if she doesn't like it. Was that the right thing to do? If not, what should I do?*

*—Club Crisis*

Wow! Your reaction to her was way harsh. You should just have explained that the majority of the club wanted the change and, therefore, it was made. Let her know you think it was the fair thing to do to go with the decision made by the majority of the group. But are you sure there's not more going on here than a disagreement about the name of a club? Take a deeper look at the situation to see if you two have other, bigger issues to deal with.

# SOCIAL SUCCESS

Wouldn't it be great if everyone at school got along perfectly? Yeah, right. That'll never happen! Bring together all different types of personalities and people, and there's bound to be conflict. Whether you're dealing with cliques or flaky friends, here's how to deal with the popularity puzzle.

*Dear Lucky,*

*In elementary school, I was popular. Now that I'm in middle school, I'm not meeting any new friends. Any ideas on how to spark up my social life?*

*—Newly Lonely*

You're probably just nervous about being in a new school. The best way to meet people, as lame as it sounds, is to be yourself. Make an effort to wave, say "hi," and start conversations with people you don't know very well. Once they realize how friendly you are, they will probably want to talk to you again. The more outgoing you are, the more people will want to get to know you.

*Dear Lucky,*

*I'm friends with girls in two different groups at school. One group is from dance class, and the other is a group of friends I've known since kindergarten. But the two groups don't get along. Should I stay friends with one group or try to make them all get along?*

*—In a Bind*

If you haven't already tried to get the girls together so that they can get to know each other better, try that. But if they already know each other and simply don't get along, it's not a good idea to force things. That doesn't mean, though, that you can't be friends with *both* groups. Who says you can't have lots of friends from different circles? Spend time with both groups separately, doing things you love to do with *each*.

## THE SECRETS TO GETTING READY ON TIME IN THE MORNING!

So you wake up at 7 a.m. for school, and you only have two minutes to get ready. You have to get dressed and eat breakfast—but you're dead tired. You don't want to go out the door like a tornado or without food in your stomach. Here are ways to cope:

❀ The night before, put whatever you need in one place. Get your clothes and backpack ready. Think about what your plans are for the whole next day. Don't forget about things you'll need after school, either—you might not have time to run home and get them. And try to remember if you promised to bring anybody anything during the day. Your best bud won't be happy if you forget the T-shirt she lent you that she needs back. So, have everything set aside and ready to go!

❀ Instead of sitting down at the breakfast table when you should be heading out the door, grab a muffin or other portable goodies, like granola bars, a bagel with cream cheese, or fruit.

❀ You should also get to bed early, and have an alarm clock to wake you up an hour before you have to leave. You could lie down at bedtime with something enjoyable to read and, when you feel your eyes drooping, put your book down and go to sleep.

—Katie D., 12

---

*Dear Lucky,*

*My BFF and I just started middle school, and things have really changed. Suddenly, she's Miss Pretty-and-Popular Cheerleader—and I'm not. Plus, she tells her new friends my secrets. Should I deal or get rid of her?*

*—Growing Apart*

Hopefully, she's going through a phase. It happens to a lot of kids when they start middle school. She's probably just trying to be accepted, which is okay. But it's *not* okay if she's losing sight of what's important—your friendship and trust. If you haven't told her you feel neglected, please do. She might not even know. Then, if she doesn't change how she treats you, make new friends and let her go her own way.

**Dear Lucky,**

*I went to a small, private elementary school, and, now, I'm about to start seventh grade at the public junior high. Because I attended such a small school, I have only a few friends. I'd really like to meet some news buds and maybe even a boyfriend (I've never had one). I'm really excited about meeting new people, but I'm pretty shy. Do you have any advice on how to introduce myself to people or start a conversation with a potential friend?*

*—Friend Needer*

Heading to a new, bigger school can seem scary at first. But there will be lots of girls in your same situation, looking for new friends and feeling nervous. You should get involved in activities and organizations you like (sports or a school club) to meet other girls with the same interests. You'll also meet new people in class. Ask a classmate a friendly question, like what she thinks about the new school. If you spot a girl eating lunch alone, see if you can join her. By the way, this advice applies to meeting that potential boyfriend, too!

**Dear Lucky,**

*I hang out with a group of friends I know from orchestra. But the other day, I heard another group of girls call us "band geeks." It really hurt my feelings and made me mad. Should I have said something to them?*

*—Music Girl*

You did the right thing by not saying anything. Otherwise, it likely would have started a big, ugly game of back-and-forth name-calling. The best way to deal is to ignore those girls. Don't, for a minute, let it get you and your friends down that some other clique labels you. In the long run, they only make themselves look bad. If you're worried about forever being referred to as "band geeks," why not come up with a clever name for your clique that'll really catch on? You know—you could be the "orchestra chicks" or something.

# CAMPUS CRISES

Not every day at school is going to be glorious. At times, you might want to hide under the nearest desk and pray for the final bell. Tricky sitches are often unavoidable, but there are ways to cope.

**Dear Lucky,**

My mom is always at my school! In chorus, she "helps out." Usually, she just sits and stares at me. That is not cool for a girl my age. I have tried to talk to her about it, but she just gets mad.

—Space Invaded

Moms never seem to get hints like, "You can just drop me off a block or two away," or, "You don't need to come to every single practice." They mean well, but it's understandable why you don't want your mom around all the time. Since you've already talked to her, try writing her a note. Explain that, while you love her and enjoy spending time with her, you also need some time with just your classmates. Maybe you can work out a compromise in which she volunteers at your school only one day a week or for classes in another grade. One more thing—your mom's probably not mad. More likely, she's hurt. Suggest a certain day of the week you two can regularly spend together to see a movie, shop, or go for ice cream. That way, she'll get that you *do* like hanging with her but that you also want her to respect some boundaries in the school setting—that's *your* scene.

**Dear Lucky,**

Help! I made a huge fool of myself at school. As I was walking into class, I tripped and fell. Everyone laughed and, now, when some of the boys see me, they pretend to trip. What am I going to do?

—Just Tripping

It's simple: Just have fun with the situation. Make light of it, and the boys in your class will be so shocked they won't know what to do. When they pretend to trip, tell them, "No, it was more like this!" Then, do a really dramatic fake trip, and say, "Ta-da!" As soon as they figure out all their teasing has no effect on you whatsoever, they'll find something else to occupy their time. If you ever trip again, just laugh it off or take a big bow.

## LAREIGN SAID IT!

### TACKLING TRYOUT TRAUMA

Whatever the sport or activity, whether it's field hockey or chorus, hundreds of thousands of girls try out for something every year. And a large number of those girls face rejection. But you can learn how to cure the "I didn't make it" blues.

*The first step* in beating this ailment is to accept the fact that you didn't make the cut. No matter how many pennies you toss in the wishing well, that won't change. It's difficult, but it has to be done. Also, don't go around complaining to everyone about how unjustly you were treated. Maybe it was unfair. Maybe you deserved to make it. But unless you want to be known as a whiner, keep the complaints to your pet poodle or write it in your private journal.

*The second step* is to know that you are not a total loser. Think of the people who didn't even have the courage to try out! It's not easy to get up in front of a judge or coach and do your thing, but you gave it your best shot and that's what's important. A single team or sport is not life. Have faith in yourself to try again because you're bound to make some team, activity, or squad someday. Beware of the attitude of "I didn't make it this time, so why should next time be any different?"

*The final step* to enduring tryout trauma is to gradually get on with your life. The key word here is "gradually." Act as you did before tryouts but not over the top. I can assure you it will be painful at times, like when you overhear a conversation about cheerleading uniforms or see a sign about softball practice. But the darkest hour is gone, and the sun is rising.

—LaReign W., 13

---

*Dear Lucky,*

*Everyone at school wears all the latest, trendiest styles. I wear loose shirts and baggy pants. I feel so out of place with my clothes. I would love to wear the right clothes to fit in, but my mom won't let me—she thinks they're indecent. What can I do?*

**—Clothes Minded**

Talk to your mom and see if you could branch out when clothes shopping. Don't expect her to allow you to wear anything you want, but hopefully she won't have a problem with *everything*. Try a new, cool skirt or top and see if she'll go for it. If you explain to your mom in the right tone of voice that you just want to fit in at school, she might understand and ease up on the restrictions.

**Dear Lucky,**

*This girl in my class spreads rumors about me! I've asked her to stop, but she won't. Can you give me any advice?*

*—Talked About*

First, ignore her. Chances are she tells tales because she gets a reaction from you. All too often, girls who don't feel great about themselves put down others to make themselves look or feel better—or so they think. If she knows her rumor-spreading upsets you, she might feel pretty powerful. If you take that power away, she'll likely get bored and move on. Keep in mind that you didn't bring this on, and it has nothing to do with you in particular. But if the rumors are especially hurtful or you feel the need to defend yourself, talk to your classmates. Set them straight by telling them the truth. Don't get super-emotional or overly defensive, though. That'll just add fuel to her fire! Just be honest, and be yourself. Your real friends will understand that the rumors are false and that this girl's gossip is bad news.

**Dear Lucky,**

*My teacher doesn't like me. She always calls on me to answer questions and, whenever a group of us is talking during class, she calls my name and not theirs. I think it's because she had my brother as a student two years ago, and he didn't do so well. Do you think I should transfer to another class?*

*—Not the Teacher's Pet*

I know what it's like to have to follow in your brother's footsteps at school! My older brother always got in trouble at school, so teachers expected me to be a huge pain—which, of course, I wasn't! You shouldn't have to pay for your brother's past behavior. Hopefully, your teacher has had you in class long enough to know you are not your brother. As for her calling on you in class, maybe she wants to challenge you to be a better student. Prove you are a star pupil by studying up and being prepared with the answers to her questions. And simply don't talk during class so she won't have to ask you to keep quiet. As long as you're doing your best, she won't have any reason to pick on you!

## YOU SAID IT!

### RULES FOR HANGING OUT WITH THE COOL GROUP

I am not the most popular girl in school, nor am I the biggest loser. But, truth be told, I hang around with the so-called cool group. And I want to share with you what I have learned:

❧ *NUMBER ONE:* Always think highly of yourself. Not too highly, but just enough and not too much. A good rule for all parts of your life, don't you think?

❧ *NUMBER TWO:* Be nice to the cool group. Don't smother them! That is *sooo* unbelievably annoying. Just smile and say "hi" if you pass them in the hall on your way to geography. If they groan and roll their eyes, so what? Then, they aren't really your friends and definitely not worth your time.

❧ *NUMBER THREE:* Try to make conversation. Like, "Do we have homework for history class?" or, "I got a new CD." Something you know you both can relate to.

❧ *NUMBER FOUR:* Don't be afraid of the popular girls! I've seen girls flinch when they see me coming. Act naturally, in a way that reveals your true self. The idea is that they like you for who you are. And if they don't, that's okay.

❧ *NUMBER FIVE:* It does help if you have something in common with the "in" group. I'm not saying redo your wardrobe or make mall trivia flashcards or cram in ten hours of taped sports events every night. Just have a common ground. If this doesn't satisfy them, maybe it isn't you at all. Maybe they only want seven people in their weekly movie trips. Hey, some kids hate change.

❧ *NUMBER SIX:* The final rule is, whatever you do, don't abandon your true friends. They are worth more than gold. You won't understand it, though, until they're gone. Remember that they never judged you because you weren't cool or you wore last week's styles. They always respected you, so don't break their trust.

—Amber N., 13

# BONUS QUIZ:

## WILL YOU BE A SCHOOL SUCCESS?

*Take this quiz to see if you know
how to make the most of your school days.*
—Amanda L., 12

**1. On the first day of school, you:**

a. find your friends and pal around with them all day.

b. hang out at the library when you have some down time to avoid all the chaos.

c. try to make friends with your new classmates.

**2. When the final bell rings, you usually:**

a. hook up with your friends to chat about the day.

b. go straight home to get your homework done.

c. head off to one of your many after-school activities.

**3. The big dance is coming up. You:**

a. plan on going and having a blast.

b. will probably sit this one out.

c. are not only going, but you're also heading up the decorations committee.

**4. Your English teacher assigns an extra credit project. You:**

a. check it out. If it won't take up too much of your time, you'll give it a go.

b. decide not to do it. You're already getting a good grade.

c. take on the challenge. A little extra credit can only help!

**5. Your Spanish class is planning a fiesta for Cinco de Mayo. You:**

a. break out your sombrero and gear up to munch on massive amounts of chips and salsa. Olé!

b. hope it's not mandatory.

c. offer to make your killer nine-layer nacho dip.

# SCORING

### Mostly A's: All About Buds

You have a great group of friends and like to spend your spare time hanging out with them. But why not also give school activities a try? Being more involved in school and activities will also help you expand your social circle!

### Mostly B's: Super Student

While you might be getting good grades, you're missing out on much, much more. Being a great student means being well-rounded, too, so take part in some of the extra-curricular activities your school offers. Joining even one club can make you feel more a part of the school experience.

### Mostly C's: Busy Buddy

You know how to make the most of your school days. Seems as if you are involved in clubs and activities and are open to new experiences. You'll likely have a great school experience and many rewarding friendships, too.

# CHAPTER 4

# GETTING INTO YOUR GROOVE

**A**lways take care of No. 1—you! When you feel confident, secure, and happy, everything else in life is much easier to deal with. Everyone gets the blues now and then, and faces hard-to-handle sitches. And that's totally normal, and just part of growing up and being a girl. Here are the answers to some of your toughest questions about being the best you can be!

# MAKING A CHANGE

Life is all about change. One day, you like red, the next, blue. Go figure! This is the time in your life to try new and different experiences so you can learn even more about yourself.

**Dear Lucky,**

*I always have trouble sticking with anything. This year, I want to play a sport. How can I make sure I don't slack off before I even get started?*

**—Slacker Girl**

Making commitments to activities, clubs, projects or whatever can be tough. Believe me—I've had my share of failed attempts. It's great you want to join an athletic team. The best way to keep on track is to do something you enjoy. Choose a sport you have fun playing, and ask a few friends to join, too! Don't get so freaked out about slacking off before you get started. Just get out there and play. If you have a good time doing it, I'll bet you'll want to stick with it!

**Dear Lucky,**

*I always get stuck doing nothing on the weekends, and it gets boring! My friends always have sports, family stuff, too much homework, etc. How can I make my weekends more interesting?*

**—Bored Silly**

Sounds as if your pals are on to something. Get out, and get involved! What interests you? Sports? Acting? Volunteering? There are tons of things you can do to make your weekends rock. Join a sports team or club that has weekend activities. Pursue a hobby like photography or karate. And what about volunteering? Spend that free time doing something good for others. Not only will you beat boredom, but you'll also realize helping people makes you feel good! Also, be proactive about your social life. Don't wait 'til Friday night to decide what to do over the weekend. Plan fun things midweek so you'll have time to make them happen.

## YOU SAID IT!

### MY ADVICE ON MAKING THE BEST OUT OF LIFE

❀ Get involved in something you love to do.

❀ Figure out how you can use your talents to help other people.

❀ Start a journal—it helps you sort out your feelings.

❀ Remember that not everyone is going to like you. That's just the way it is.

❀ Keep friends who respect you for who you are.

❀ When entering a contest, never think, "Oh, I'll never win." You *can* win.

❀ Do your best to be a good person, and don't whine.

❀ Meditate.

❀ Always be open to constructive criticism—you might improve yourself.

❀ Choose your arguments carefully.

❀ Be sensitive to others' feelings.

❀ Learn a new vocabulary word every day.

❀ Stand up straight. It makes you look more confident.

❀ You are beautiful. Know that.

❀ Don't treat bad moods like the end of the world. Bad moods happen to everybody, not just you.

❀ Be happy with your looks.

❀ Focus on the good things. Don't look for the bad in everything.

❀ Be thankful for everything you have.

❀ Respect your parents. They love you.

—Emmy M., 13

*Dear Lucky,*

*I feel out of place lately, and I find it harder to strike up a conversation and make new friends. I feel really stupid and uncomfortable. Any suggestions?*

**—Nothing to Say**

Everybody gets in a rut sometimes. It can be hard to work up the courage to speak up and make conversation with people you don't know well. Quash those nerves, and dig up that friendly, outgoing self from inside you. Volunteer to organize something for a group you're involved with, or ask someone new to partner up in gym class. You're sure to meet people and feel more involved in things. If you can't figure out what to say, look for things you might have in common with someone, like the song that girl keeps humming, the animal rights sticker on her notebook, or the cool flared jeans she's wearing. Starting with something trivial or serving up a compliment can often get a conversation rolling.

*Dear Lucky,*

*I seem to forget things lately, like doing my chores when I'm supposed to or getting my homework done on time. Help!*

**—Forgetful One**

Sounds as though you need a planner or organizer! Check out planners at a stationery store—there are a ton of cute ones in lots of different styles. Use the "To Do" section to make lists of things you need to do (like those chores!). Use the calendar to jot down important dates, like test days or club meetings. Keep your planner in your backpack so you'll have it when you need it. If a planner really isn't your style, use a pad of paper or index cards to write down a daily list of things you have to do. Spend a few minutes every morning, or at night if that works better for you, writing down what you need to get done the next day. Having everything written out should help you remember.

# JUST BE YOU!

Does it always seem as if you're struggling to figure out who you really are and trying to decide what's right for you? Get to know yourself—and appreciate who you really are—no matter what! Here are some suggestions.

**Dear Lucky,**

*Recently, I've felt really lonely and that nobody likes me. I've been trying to hang with the popular group, but they don't pay attention to me.*

*—Lonely*

Why are you limiting yourself to the "popular" group? Strike up a conversation with that cool girl behind you in class—the one who might not be the most popular but seems like a bunch of fun. Inquire about a homework assignment, an extra-curricular activity, or even a cute boy. Hanging with the popular crowd might seem like the way to go, but you should look for real friends—girls who share the same interests as you and who you can really connect with. Maybe you won't feel so lonely once you find a friend who likes you for you.

**Dear Lucky,**

*My friends make fun of me because I don't like the same music they like. They say I listen to "old people" music because it's stuff our parents listen to. But I don't like the music my friends like. What should I do?*

*—Music Confused*

Don't change who you are or what you like for your friends! If they're your friends, no doubt you share a lot of common interests, like clothing styles, movies, or even who you crush on. But no two people are exactly alike—and no way could you and your pals like all the same things. Case in point: your music interests. Don't get worked up when they give you a hard time. Simply say, "Hey! At least you don't have to worry about me borrowing your CDs and never returning them!" Make light of it, and then move on to a topic of interest you share, like the new movie you've all been dying to see.

## LAURA SAID IT!

### WHO ARE YOU?

Since you're at an age when you are changing, it's time to think about who you want to be in the future. Is the kind of person you are right now a good start for being the person you wish to be? Growing up is easier if you've established values and know what is important in life. Set goals, and follow your role models. When you do that, you'll have confidence.

Don't refrain from trying new things just because you're afraid you'll fail. Develop your talents and skills to your fullest potential. Think about how much you love your family. Think of how proud they'll be when you work hard. Always listen when someone wise speaks, and think about what they're saying. Be open to new ideas, and question the things you have been taught.

Growing up is tough and full of tricky sitches. Just remember that what is popular is not always right, and what is right is not always popular. Do what you know is right, and you will realize what is truly important in life. You'll be able to deal with large important problems, and you will be less bothered by small unimportant issues. Confidently strive to be who you want to be, and you will become a shining star.

—Laura N., 15

*Dear Lucky,*

*I want to become a vegetarian because I think eating animals is so gross! But my mom says, "No way." How can I get her to change her mind?*

—*Ready to Veg*

One word, two syllables: Research. Don't just tell her eating meat is icky. Get the scoop on skipping meat so you can show your mom you can still grow healthy and strong without it. Your mom probably thinks that if you stop eating meat you'll miss out on some important nutrients and vitamins. She could have a point, so you really should talk to your doctor before deciding to go veggie. Your physician can help you plan a nutritional eating regimen and recommend some vitamins. I think the more you and your mom know about vegetarianism, the better she'll feel about helping you make this decision.

**Dear Lucky,**

*I don't like rides or anything that goes fast, but my friends go on a lot of trips to water and amusement parks. I don't want to just sit there bored while everyone else goes on rides. What can I do?*

**—Scaredy Cat**

Luckily, there are tons of not-so-scary things to do at amusement parks! Why not go on the bumper cars, ferris wheel, or swings instead? At the water park, you can swim and go on the (slow) lazy river tube ride. You can also play games, grab fun food, and see cool shows with animals and stunt people. Bottom line: Don't worry about being bored. There's little chance of that happening at any amusement park!

# YOU—INSIDE AND OUT

Take a look around you. Unless you live on a different planet, what you'll see is a mix of girls and boys of all different shapes, sizes, and colors. Which is best? Even you know that's a silly question. How you or anyone else looks is of little importance. It's what's on the inside that matters most!

**Dear Lucky,**

*This past summer, I had to get braces. I hate them! I feel so ugly with them, and the orthodontist says I have to wear them for another year. What am I going to do?*

**—Brace Face**

Take it from someone who also had to wear braces for over a year—they take some getting used to, but braces are definitely not ugly. In fact, you're part of a pretty big club. Tons of kids have braces. They're practically a fashion statement at some schools. A year might seem like a long time, but it'll fly by, and next thing you know, you'll be heading to the ortho to have them removed. And, then you can flash your new smile non-stop!

> **Dear Lucky,**
>
> *I feel really fat sometimes, especially in the summer. I hate wearing shorts or bathing suits. What can I do?*
>
> *—Feeling Fat*

It's worth repeating—it really doesn't matter what you look like on the outside. It's how you feel on the inside that counts. Be comfortable with how you look, and wear clothes that flatter your body type. Try a cute tankini. Or how about buying some capris, instead of shorty-shorts? And try working out and eating right. Summer is a great time to swim, take walks, and ride your bike. You'll feel better and more energized. Also, if you eat more healthful foods, you'll really feel better. So eat more fruits, and veggies, and go for snacks like frozen yogurt and pretzels. And, if you have great self-esteem, it'll shine through to others.

> **Dear Lucky,**
>
> *I'm 12 years old and five-foot-ten. I really don't mind, except when this creepy boy teases me and calls me rude names. I even told a teacher and my parents about it, but nothing has been done. What else can I do?*
>
> *—Too Tall*

It's great that you're happy with your height—being tall definitely has its advantages! This boy probably feels a little insecure because you're taller than he is. Still, that doesn't give him the right to be rude to you! Ignore all the name-calling—if he doesn't get a reaction from you, he's likely to stop. If he doesn't stop, go back to your teacher and parents and explain how important this situation is to you, so they can help put a stop to it.

**Dear Lucky,**

*I have a disability, so I feel like no boy could ever like me as more than a friend. I just can't help thinking boys deserve better, someone "normal." How can I shake these negative feelings?*

*—Putting Off Boys*

No way does having a disability make you abnormal. You sure aren't alone. Maybe you're not like everyone else, but maybe that's exactly what some special boy will like about you one day. I'm sure you are fun, energetic, and smart—qualities that really matter. Once you realize how amazing you are, others will see that, too.

**Dear Lucky,**

*I want to look good this school year, but I hate makeup. How can I look nice without a lot of makeup?*

*—Clean Faced*

How about trying a different hairstyle? A new haircut could be just the thing to make you feel better. Or, you could get a new outfit or two—go for a style you've never worn before. Bottom line: You don't need makeup to give yourself a makeover!

**Dear Lucky,**

*I have a face full of freckles, and I hate them. I have them on my chest and arms, too. How can I get rid of them— or at least hide them from view?*

*—Freckle Face*

It's so true that we all want what we don't have and don't want what we do have. Case in point: I always wanted freckles. I think they're super-cute, and so do a lot of other people. Trying to conceal them with makeup is not a good idea. Your freckles are a part of you, so embrace them—they're part of what makes you you. It'd be pretty strange for people to all of a sudden see you freckle-free, don't ya think? And if you're just feeling the urge for a new look, alter something that *can* be changed— like get a new hairstyle or a cute new outfit.

# DEALING WITH TRICKY SITCHES

While most everyday problems aren't too unbearable, at times you'll face tougher issues. Here's some help for hard-to-handle situations.

*Dear Lucky,*

*This girl at school makes fun of me and even hits me. I've told her to stop, but she won't. I'm fed up with it. How can I fight back?*

**—Fed Up**

You need to put a stop to this ASAP. Verbal abuse and physical harassment should never be tolerated. You definitely don't want to fight back—that would just make things blow up even more. Since you've asked her to stop and she won't, let someone else know what's going on. Talk to your principal, guidance counselor, or teacher. Also, make sure your parents know what's happening. You shouldn't put up with this. This girl is probably treating you poorly because of her own insecurities—it's not your fault at all.

## YOU SAID IT!

### STRESS BUSTERS!

Big test coming up? Trouble with friends? Always busy? If this sounds anything like your life, remember that you're not alone! With these tips, you could find yourself back on the road to total happiness and sanity.

❀ *SMILE!* Even when you're feeling down and out, you'll find that a simple smile will make you and the people around you feel more cheerful. How? When you smile, other people smile back at you and your brain registers the happy look and works on other happy responses, like easing tension in your body and calming your heart rate down. So when you freeze up, smile away your stress.

❀ *STAY OPTIMISTIC!* When things seem really bad, look on the bright side.

❀ *REMEMBER THE GOOD STUFF!* When you're upset, think of all the good you've done and all the people you've helped.

❀ *TALK!* Tell your friends and family what's on your mind. Don't be afraid to ask for advice or help when you don't have a solution to every issue. Involving others in solving your problems not only creates more solutions, but it also helps you come up with your own answers. Communication is the key!

—Jamie D., 13

## YOU SAID IT!

### WHY IT'S CHIC TO BE A GEEK

I'm proud to call myself a "dork." (I actually *like* to stay home with my folks on Friday nights.) But being a dork does not mean I'm a loser. Loserdom and dorkdom are entirely different categories. As a full-fledged dork, my phone rings frequently, I play softball and tennis, and I love to folk dance—all of which prevent me from qualifying as a loser. A loser is someone who has no drive. I'm tired of people assuming it's better to be part of the "cool" group. It's time for the dorks of the world to unite and realize how cool we really are.

First, let me explain why it really *is* better to be a dork. As a self-proclaimed dork, I have absolutely nothing to hide. I know I'm not hip and trendy—and that my friends love me for who I am, not who I pretend to be. When you don't feel you have to prove yourself, you have freedom to focus on activities you actually enjoy. Does anyone really like making others uncomfortable by acting like a snob or being loud and obnoxious in the back of the bus? Probably not—and as a dork, I can sit quietly in the middle of the bus and read, or pretend to read while I think about how glad I am to be me.

Because I don't have to spend a lot of time worrying about my social status or sweating over getting my hands on the "right" clothes, I can focus on things that are important to me—like improving my musical skills and spending time with my dorky friends. When you are in the company of lots of dorks, you realize that, hey, being a dork is cool. My phone rings a lot because my friends realize that people who study and play instruments are far more interesting than people who put their energy into maintaining a high social standing.

As you get older, being a dork becomes even more beneficial. The dorkier you are, the better job you might get—because you work hard. If you *do* happen to be a snobby "cool" person, you might want to change your attitude. You know the smart girl who knows all the answers in history? She just might be your boss one day!

—Kim P., 13

**Dear Lucky,**

*Ever since we moved to a new town, I feel sad. I don't have any friends yet, and my parents are too busy to even notice me. I don't know what to do or who to talk to.*

*—In a Funk*

Moving to a new town is tough. You have to make a whole new set of friends, and everything is unfamiliar. It takes time. You can speed up the process by getting involved in activities. Were you in a sport or club at your old school? Sign up for something similar in your new town. Also, volunteer to help with school events or community activities. Check out the town's recreation department for classes and events. Or, indulge in your favorite hobby at home, like baking or scrapbooking. Your parents might *seem* too busy to notice you, but I'll bet if you talk to them about how you feel, they'll listen and offer advice. And you can always e-mail one of your old friends for some cheering up.

**Dear Lucky,**

*My cat got really sick, and we had to put her to sleep. I am so sad that I don't even want to go to school or be around my friends. My parents think I am overreacting.*

*—Cat Lover*

It's very painful to lose a pet, and of course, you're sad. It takes time to get over a loss, but it will get a little easier every day. Even though you don't want to be around your friends right now, you'll feel better to get out and do fun things. Friends can help you get through this. You might not think they understand what you're going through, and maybe none of them *have* ever lost a pet, but friends should want to comfort you and cheer you up. If it's all right with your parents, consider getting a new cat soon— it's almost impossible to be sad around a playful kitten.

*Dear Lucky,*

*My dad recently lost his job. I am really worried about what's going to happen to us. My parents don't talk to me much about what is going on, so that makes me even more scared. What should I do?*

*—Confused Daughter*

A parent's job loss can be tough on everyone in the family. But don't think that just because your parents are not communicating with you that something awful is going to happen. They are probably keeping quiet because they don't want you to worry…like you are doing now. Just tell them how you're feeling. If they know you're scared, they might be more open about what is going on. Also, let them know you are willing to help out in any way you can. Families have to stick together when the going gets tough! If they still don't feel comfortable chatting with you about their adult matters, talk to a close friend or adult you can trust, like a school counselor or someone at your community center. You'll feel better just getting things off your chest.

# YOU SAID IT!

## DEALING WITH BEING DIFFERENT

I have some advice for girls who are "different." Don't follow the crowd. I know you've heard it way too much, but it's true. I used to be unpopular because I was different, but then some other people broke away from the crowd, too. So now we're all friends, and we're all pretty popular without sacrificing our personalities. So, like I said, be yourself and hang in there. Decent people can appreciate differences— and who wants mean friends?

—Katie L., 13

# BONUS QUIZ:

## WHAT KIND OF PERSON ARE YOU?

*Are you a good citizen, a bad egg, or do you fall somewhere in between? Take this quiz to find out how you measure up on the Good Samaritan meter.*

—Jamie E., 12

1. **You see an elderly woman fall and have a hard time getting up by herself. You:**

    a. rush over and help her.

    b. think, "She's too heavy to lift."

    c. yell, "Someone, help this person!"

2. **Someone asks you to help out at the local food drive on Friday night. You don't have anything planned, so you say:**

    a. "Sorry, I can't possibly miss my favorite TV show."

    b. "Maybe my cousin Carla could help you."

    c. "What time should I be there?"

3. **You go shopping with a friend, and she asks for your opinion on the dress she just tried on. You think it looks horrible on her. You say:**

    a. "Gross. Put it back before someone sees you."

    b. "Ask the clerk. I just found the perfect dress for myself."

    c. "Try something a little brighter to match your personality."

4. **You go to a pool party wearing a totally funky swimsuit. Your friend isn't so lucky. She walks up to you, and you:**

    a. say, "Get lost. You look terrible!"

    b. say, "Hi! That swimsuit doesn't look the best on you. Would you like to borrow one of mine?"

    c. walk in the other direction—fast.

**5. Your mom wants you to wash the dishes. You don't want to, so you:**

    a. have a fit and yell your head off.

    b. say, "Where's the dish detergent?"

    c. say, "Maybe Katie can do it. I'm busy filing my nails."

# SCORING

**1. a. 3, b. 1, c. 2**

**2. a. 1, b. 2, c. 3**

**3. a. 1, b. 2, c. 3**

**4. a. 1, b. 3, c. 2**

**5. a. 1, b. 3, c. 2**

**12 to 15 points: Good Samaritan**
You are a very helpful person. Keep up the good work. But beware of being too helpful—sometimes it annoys people.

**9 to 11 points: Lazy Lady**
You love to get other people to do your work. Try to do some yourself.

**5 to 8 points: Bad Egg**
Be nice! You like to say things that hurt people—lighten up a little.

# CHAPTER 5

# SETTING YOUR
# HEART STRAIGHT

**E**ven if you haven't had your first crush yet, trust me—you'll know when the crush bug hits! Chances are you'll spend countless hours chatting about your crush with your BFF. Between trying to figure out *his* feelings and dealing with your *own*, crushes can be majorly confusing.

Fear not, though, because if you have the right attitude about boys, "crush time" can be one of the most exciting times of your young life. Here's help for your basic boy issues.

# TAKING THE PLUNGE

So...who do you have a crush on? If you blush just thinking about him, you clearly have been bitten by the crush bug. But now what? Read on to find out.

*Dear Lucky,*
*Whenever I'm friends with a guy, I start to like him as more than just a friend. What's my problem?*

**—Always Crushing**

Aaargh! Plenty of girls are in the same sitch. Remind yourself that not every guy is a potential boyfriend. When you get to know a boy as a friend, all you should expect out of the relationship is a buddy to hang out with (which is often a lot better than having a boyfriend). Know what you want out of the relationship from the beginning. If you have a crush on someone, don't try to be all buddy-buddy with him. But if you meet a guy you just want to be friends with, keep it that way from the start.

*Dear Lucky,*
*Is 11 too young to have a crush?*

**—Wondering**

It depends. Only you really know the answer to that one. There are some things to think about: Why do you want to have a crush? Is it because you met a great boy who's super nice, fun to be around, and a total cutie? Or is it because your BFF has a boyfriend? If it's the latter, that's not a good reason. But, if you have met a boy, gotten to know him, and like him—and if you think he likes you too—then crush away.

**Dear Lucky,**

*I have the biggest crush on my camp counselor, but I'm 11 and he's 15. I think he has a pretty good idea I like him. Should I do anything?*

—*The Younger Girl*

It's okay to admire your counselor and think he's cute—like you would if you had a celebrity crush. However, and I know it's not what you want to hear, that's really as far as it goes. There's a major age difference between you. Even if you're totally mature and look 15, you are 11. This is real life, so keep your starry-eyed thoughts in check and concentrate on crushing on other campers your own age.

**Dear Lucky,**

*I really like this boy at my school, but I am too shy to talk to him. I don't think he knows who I am. But if I were to go up and just start talking to him, I think that would look dumb. I'd send a friend to do it, but the last two times I did that my friends ended up liking the boys I asked them to talk to! I'm only shy around boys I like. I can talk to other boys with no problem. Please, help.*

—*Shy Girl*

Guess you learned the hard way not to have your friends do the talking for you! But talking to a boy you like can be nerve-racking, especially when you don't know him that well. Here are a few ideas, though, to help you break the ice:

❀ Approach him by yourself. Sometimes it's easier to untie your tongue when your classmates and friends are nowhere to be found.

❀ Approach him when he's with a mutual friend. Surely, you know someone he knows. When you spot them together, head on over and say "hello."

❀ Don't let an opportunity pass you by. Next time he passes you in the hall, smile and say "hello" the second your eyes meet. He's bound to take notice.

Good luck!

**Dear Lucky,**

*My boyfriend moved, so we broke up. But I still think about him all the time. Now, this boy at school likes me, and I think I like him. Should I hang out with this new boy or daydream forever about my old BF?*

—***Torn***

Since you and your boyfriend broke up, give this new boy a chance—especially since you seem to like him. There's no rule that says you can't think about your old BF, but try to move on. You'll have more fun building a relationship with someone you can actually spend time with. Living in the past is a drag.

**Dear Lucky,**

*I have a major crush on this guy in math class. I think he is super nice and cute, but my friends don't see him that way. They think he's geeky, and they make fun of me when I hang out with him. I really like him, but I don't want to upset my buds. What can I do?*

—***Confused About My Crush***

If you really like this guy, don't worry about what your friends think! You have the right to like and hang out with anyone you want to, and your friends don't have to approve. Explain to your friends how you feel about him. Let them know you really like this guy and that it hurts your feelings when they put him down. Ask them to get to know him before judging him—and, if he is as awesome as you think he is, your friends should grow to like him, too. If they continue to make fun, you might want to consider finding more supportive friends.

# HE LIKES ME...HE LIKES ME NOT

You'll probably spend more time trying to figure this one out than solving your toughest geometry problem! But here are some tips to help you tell if he likes you or *likes* you.

*Dear Lucky,*

*I'm afraid my BF is losing interest in me. How can I be sure of his feelings?*

*—Unsure*

Before you jump to conclusions, maybe there's a logical explanation. Is he stressing over super-tough classes, team tryouts, or personal stuff? He might just be focused on things other than you, and is so busy he doesn't realize he's skimping on time with you. Just because he's not all ga-ga, it doesn't necessarily mean he's lost interest. Also, maybe he's worried you're the one who's lost interest. Test the waters first to get an idea as to where he stands—invite him to join you at the skating rink or pizza parlor Friday night. If he's psyched, cool! But if he makes ridiculous excuses, it might be time to move on.

*Dear Lucky,*

*I like this boy who takes lessons from my piano teacher. I met him at our recital, and he seemed to like me. He goes to an all-boys school, and I think it would be too forward of me to call him. But I don't want to sit back and do nothing. Any suggestions?*

*—Missing Him*

There's nothing wrong with calling him, so dial him up. He might be really excited and appreciative that you had the guts to pick up the phone. When you do call, make the conversation casual so you don't come off too forward. Invite him to a movie with you and your friends, and suggest he bring a few friends along. That way, you two can comfortably hang out and get to know one another.

**Dear Lucky,**

*I have a guy who's a friend. At least, I think he's my friend. He recently told me he has a crush on me. But I just want to be friends. I told him that, and he got mad and ran away. What should I do?*

*—Just a Bud*

I don't think he's mad. He's probably embarrassed. It took a lot of guts for him to tell you what he really feels, and, when things didn't turn out as he'd hoped, well, he felt a little mortified. Give him some time, and play it cool when you're around him. Show him that you're still the same friend he's always had and that you won't let this revelation ruin your friendship. If he is truly a friend, he'll come around.

**Dear Lucky,**

*I just found out that the guy I've been crushing on has a crush on me, too. Now what?!*

*—Needing the Next Step*

So now he likes you and all the little butterflies you've had fluttering around in your stomach have turned into...*big* butterflies. Don't worry—it's not so bad! Spending more time with him and getting to know him will be part of the fun. I suggest you go up and talk to him. Ask him how his science project is going, or even suggest that you go to a school function together. Once you get the conversation rolling, it'll be easier. You two will probably get in some phone and hang time, and one day—maybe soon—you'll realize you have a BF!

**Dear Lucky,**

*I like this boy who told me he likes me a lot. But, then, he told his friends he doesn't like me just because they don't like me. I don't understand why he's doing this. Is he worth my time?*

—**Duped**

He's acting immature. A lot of boys (and some girls, too, for that matter) do what their friends think is cool instead of what they want to do. He probably likes you, but since, for whatever reason, his friends don't like you, he won't be honest about his feelings. He could also be embarrassed to tell his friends he likes you because they might tease him. Next time you see him and no friends are around, ask him what's going on. If he says he likes you and then he treats you well, he could be worth your time. If he acts weird toward you, whether or not his friends are around, he's probably too immature for you right now.

# ALL ABOUT THE BOY BRAIN

When it comes to understanding boys, boy-oh-boy are there a lot of theories! If you're having trouble figuring out what boys are all about, read on for some assistance.

**Dear Lucky,**

*My BF wants to kiss me. We are only 12. What should I do?*

—**Kiss Confused**

First of all, if you don't feel comfortable with something, you shouldn't do it. If you're not ready to kiss him, don't. Explain to your boyfriend how you feel, and ask him to respect your feelings. He should understand.

**Dear Lucky,**

*I've liked the same boy since second grade. While walking me home from school the other day, he tried to kiss me. I told him to stop, and he got really mad and left. I still like him. Should I apologize?*

**—Confused**

You did the right thing! If anyone does something that makes you uncomfortable, you should speak up. If he really likes you, he'll respect you and your decisions. I don't think you owe this boy an apology. He owes *you* an apology! But now that you know he likes you, maybe you two can use your lips to talk about your feelings for each other.

## YOU SAID IT!

### HOW TO TELL IF A BOY LIKES YOU

Okay, I have done this before, and it works. If you want to know if a guy likes you, you have to be sly. You need to talk to him more and more every day. If you say "hi" to him in the hall, the next day you should say "hi" again and try to strike up a short convo. Do this every day or so until you can work up to longer conversations.

During one of these convos, ask him what he is doing over the weekend, or tell him where you and your friends will be hanging out and ask if he would like to join you. If he gets the message, he will hang around you more often. If he doesn't, he will think you just wanted to be friendly. I hope this works for you!

—Lissa, 13

**Dear Lucky,**

*My BFF is a boy, and other boys don't express any interest in me because they assume he's my BF. I don't want to end our friendship, but I'd like the chance to have a BF. What should I do?*

**—Bummed About Boys**

Having a boy BFF is great! Your other good friends—boys and girls—must know you two don't date. Or do they? People might assume you two are boyfriend and girlfriend. When you hang with a group, don't stick together in a cozy corner. Circulate. If he walks up while you're talking to someone, introduce him as your good friend. When people ask if he's your BF, let them know the deal. Sorry, but the burden is on you to bust the myth that this boy's your BF.

**Dear Lucky,**

*I have a crush on this cutie, and he is well aware of it. So when my best guy friend asked me to the homecoming dance, I told him I would think about it. The next day, my crush invited me! Who should I go with?*

*—In a Dance Dilemma*

An invite from a crush is often too much to resist. But protecting your friendship with your friend is important, too. Friends come before boys, even when friends are boys. When new emotions enter the boy-girl friendship field, tread lightly. Does your guy friend want a dance buddy or a date? Is he crushing on you? If there's a chance you could feel the same, accept his offer. If the feeling isn't mutual, be honest. Tell him your friendship is way more important than taking that risk, and suggest he invite someone else. Ideally, your guy friend should be stoked for you that your crush asked you to the dance! If this is all too much to process for now, do the polite thing and accept your guy friend's offer. After all, he asked first. A potential crush should respect your loyalty when you explain that you already agreed to go with a friend.

**Dear Lucky,**

*I have a new BF, but he says he doesn't "want to become inseparable." We have a great time talking together on the phone and e-mailing, but we never really spend time together. How can I change his mind?*

*—Miss My BF*

Hmm. If he's your BF, he should want to hang out with you, right? Talking on the phone and e-mailing don't exactly qualify as spending quality time together. It's okay if he wants some space, but it sounds like he has plenty of breathing room and still doesn't make time to be with you—and that's not cool. Did you agree with him at first that you didn't want to be "inseparable," but now your feelings have evolved? If so, explain that you have had a change of heart and would like to do more things together—suggest bowling, a movie, a bike ride in the park. Who knows? He might feel the same way. Maybe he's been protecting himself by keeping his distance. If you get the impression he doesn't want to make any changes to his schedule, backtrack and try being his friend. If that doesn't fly, you might be happier going solo!

## YOU SAID IT!

### SHOULD YOU GO FOR THAT CRUSH?

It all started at a school dance. I had a major crush on this guy in chorus (I mean *major*, like I went three times to the play he had a minor role in!). Of course, all my friends knew and teased me about it. At our school dance, they asked him to dance with me. I hid behind a friend while this was going on, practically dying. When they came back, they said he had no clue who I was. I was so embarrassed that I almost ran out of the dance. But my real friends went back and asked him again, and he said "yes!" I flipped out—I was so excited.

When it came to that "special dance," we just stood there until our friends pushed us toward each other. Well, I guess I was thinking too much because neither of us talked during the whole dance. After we danced, we joked around and stuff, but I really didn't feel comfortable around him. I felt like I had to impress him the whole time. That was the trouble. On the last slow dance, he asked me to dance again, and I accepted. When I left the dance, I could feel the excitement bubbling up inside me. "The boy of my dreams," I thought to myself.

But when we got back to school the following week, something was wrong. We hardly talked to each other. We'd pass in the hallways and... nothing. Of course, our friends joked and made us talk to each other, but we were always uptight. You're probably thinking how stupid that is. But when you talk to a boy you've had a crush on for so long, you sort of imagined what he would be like, and it's hard when he is not like you thought he would be.

While watching TV one day, I was interrupted by the phone ringing. I picked up and mumbled "hello." When I heard his voice, my heart jumped. I listened while he explained that he thought he was too young to have a girlfriend. This really got me thinking. I came to the decision that *I* was too young as well. I was not ready. So, now, I'm okay with it. I don't want a boyfriend and, if I ever get one, I want to be older and have the confidence to handle it. So, maybe you should not be so eager for that crush to notice you. It's okay to admire him from afar. No need to rush it.

—Annie S., 14

# "HELP! NO GUYS LIKE ME!"

Do you feel as though you're the only girl who's never had a BF? Before you think so, stay confident. One day, someone will appreciate all your super characteristics and fall for you big-time. Promise!

## Dear Lucky,

*I go to boy-girl parties and dances a lot. I'm popular and nice, but no boys seem to like me! If I tell a guy I like him, he always says, "Ew, I don't like you." Why don't boys ever want to dance with girls like me?*

**—Unliked**

First off, could you be exaggerating? I can't imagine any guy reacting like that. If so, "Ew! He is totally obnoxious!" Don't give a guy like that another thought, and cut yourself some slack. Could the boys you approach be nervous? School dances are weird like that. Even the most social guys and girls get a little freaked at these gigs—even if they don't seem to be breaking a sweat. Instead of lingering on the sidelines, get in there! Chat and laugh it up with some cute boys. Or invite that cutie to groove with you and your friends. Just relax and have fun. Don't put so much pressure on yourself or on the guys. Dances are supposed to be fun—so have some!

## Dear Lucky,

*I hate Valentine's Day! All my friends have boyfriends, and I don't. What can I do to make sure February 14th isn't a total dud?*

**—BF-less**

Valentine's Day is a great day—with or without a boyfriend. Don't sweat it that you don't have a BF—have fun with your friends and family. Make super-creative glitter valentines for all your pals, wear red and white, and have a good time being silly. Surely, you aren't the only one without a BF! Invite your friends who don't have sweeties for an evening of watching romantic comedies on DVD. If you truly are the only gal without a dude, make a date with your mom or sis. Don't take this one little holiday so seriously. Plenty of mushy, gushy Valentine's Days are in your future. Meantime, devour some candy hearts and enjoy!

## Boy Crazy or Just Crazy?

Are you sick of hearing your friends whine about wanting a BF? Me too. I am tired of reassuring my friends they'll meet some cool boy one day. Do boys reassure each other they will someday find Miss Right? No. Why not? Because boys are encouraged to be independent while girls are shown—on TV, in movies, and magazines—that a boyfriend is the key to total happiness.

I'm not saying having or wanting a BF is wrong. I've hung out with guys who were positive additions to my life. What bothers me is the amount of time, attention, and energy my friends spend worrying about boys. An example? One of my friends recently told me, "I need a new boy to be obsessed with. I want to be excited about someone. Who should it be?"

Although this might seem extreme, my friend is not unique. While I see boys feeling totally satisfied hanging with their friends, doing after-school activities and playing sports, many girls yearn for more—a boyfriend. The message to "hurry up and find a boyfriend" can be found in the movies we flock to, the TV shows we tune into, and the magazines we read.

No wonder my friends think they need a boyfriend to be normal. But I'm not buying it. I can't help but think the media teaches us to put boys first. And I think it's time we take a stand against those outdated notions. Girls should feel they have qualities within themselves—independent of crushes—that bring ultimate happiness. Playing sports or acting in the school play can teach you about your inner talents and strengths. Finding an activity you love is infinitely more gratifying and stable than a romance. Healthy relationships with boys can add happiness to your life but should not be the core of it. If you are emotionally invested in activities, you'll not only learn more about your talents and ambitions but will also avoid feeling you need a boyfriend to validate who you are. Now, that's girl power!

—Kimberly P., 15

**Dear Lucky,**

*Why do boys only like skinny girls? I am a little bit bigger than a few of my friends, but boys treat me like I am inferior just because I am a little bit bigger. It really gets me down. Can you explain why guys act the way they do about the size of girls and don't focus on their feelings? It would really help to clear a few things up.*

—Needing An Answer

Boys are always a few steps behind girls when it comes to the maturity factor. Notice how some boys never seem to stop acting like they're in first grade? This is a common pattern, and it explains a lot. Boys who are not yet mature tend not to recognize that girls of all shapes can be attractive, funny, and interesting. The boys you know sound particularly immature since they treat you like you're inferior. Unfortunately, you can't order boys to grow up and focus on important things, like a girl's personality. You just have to wait for them to get there someday. In the meantime, if you're feeling down, remind yourself of all the wonderful things about you. When these boys *do* grow up, they'll hopefully realize how silly they were for not noticing your wonderful attributes sooner.

# LIKING THE SAME BOY

Nothing seems to cause friend friction quite as much as boy problems—especially when you and a pal like the same boy. If you always fall for your friend's crushes—or vice versa—I've got some sensible tips on how to deal.

**Dear Lucky,**

*For some reason, every time any one of my friends has a crush on a guy, I like him, too. Am I just jealous?*

—Crushing Too Much

It could be that you're jealous, not that you actually start to like your friends' crushes the second they do. When a friend crushes on someone new, maybe it reminds you that you would like to have a crush, too. This jealousy could be expressed by developing a teeny-tiny crush on a friend's boy of choice. Strike up a conversation with the cute boy behind you in the lunch line or the funny boy in your gym class instead. Maybe you'll find someone *you* like.

**Dear Lucky,**

*This boy and girl were going out for a long time. They broke up, and he likes me now. I like him, too, but this girl is kind of my friend. She still likes him, even though he doesn't like her anymore. I can't help who I like, can I?*

**—Third Wheel**

If you are really friends with this girl, crushing on someone she still has feelings for is a bad idea unless you're prepared to kiss the friendship goodbye. The big question is whether you can live with the fact that liking him will probably end your relationship with her. Think long and hard about it. Relationships with boys don't usually last forever, but true friendships can.

**Dear Lucky,**

*My friend and I have a crush on the same boy. We both promised that if he asked one of us out, we'd say "no." So he was flirting with me a lot—holding my hand and calling me—but then he asked out my friend. And she said "yes!" Now, I'm really upset. Why did she do this to me?*

**—Betrayed**

I understand why you're upset, and you have a right to be. If she really likes him, that's okay. But she shouldn't have agreed to a promise she wasn't willing to keep. Explain to your friend that you are hurt that she went back on her word. Let her know that, if she really likes this boy, you will be happy for her, but that you are upset she broke a pact with you. Hopefully, she will realize why you are hurt. Let it go, and move on with your life. Friends make mistakes, and there are plenty of other boys to crush on.

It's not the end of the world when another girl likes the same boy you like. Tell her you like him, too. It will give you guys something to talk about, and it could be fun to have someone to gawk at him with. Relax, and don't get jealous before anything even happens. Take this opportunity to bond and get to know her better. It seems like you two have something in common already, so expand on that and don't worry about the boy. All of that will work out in the end.

## YOU SAID IT!

### 18 THINGS YOU SHOULDN'T SAY TO YOUR CRUSH

1. "I enjoy staring at you!"
2. "I love the socks you wore last Monday."
3. "Hey, do you like these earrings I bought to impress you?"
4. "Did you see how cute Justin looks today?"
5. "I prank-called you the other night. Did you know it was me?"
6. "My mom loves your haircut."
7. "I'm your biggest fan."
8. "How come you didn't ask me to the dance?"
9. "I lost my watch. Can I borrow yours?"
10. "My dad wants to meet you."
11. "I got us tickets to the opera."
12. "I think Gretchen is jealous now that you and I are an item."
13. "Do you even know my name?"
14. "My sister baked you a birthday cake."
15. "Do you have even one bit of interest in me?"
16. "Hey, Joe, I mean, Jason. Sorry."
17. "I have to report back to the mothership soon."
18. "I framed your yearbook picture, and I kiss it every night."

—Aliza A., 12; Maggie E., 13; Bailey L., 14; Theresa L., 12; Colleen O., 13; Amy P., 12; Diane P., 13

# CALLING IT QUITS

Breaking up is hard to do, but sometimes it's the best thing to do. When you grow apart from someone or realize a boy's behavior isn't crush-worthy, you might need to move on. Or, he might end things with you for whatever reason. Either way, it's tough. But you *can* cope.

**Dear Lucky,**

*My BF told his friend he thinks the new girl at school is pretty. Is he going to dump me?*

**—Nervous**

Just because your boyfriend thinks the new girl is pretty doesn't mean he's going to dump you. It means he's a normal guy who notices girls and talks to his friends about it. It doesn't mean he thinks she's prettier than you or that he wants to go out with her. Don't make more of it than what it is. Be honest—don't you notice when a new guy is cute? That doesn't mean you like your BF any less. However, if he obsesses over other girls or he shamelessly flirts, then consider dumping *him*!

**Dear Lucky,**

*Is it wrong to break up with your BF because you like another boy?*

**—Puzzled**

Okay, there are two issues here. First, you need to decide if you want to break up with your BF. Does he respect you? Do you have fun together? Do you still get butterflies in your stomach when he walks in a room? If things are still all good, there might not be a reason to end it. You're human, and it's perfectly normal to notice other cuties. If you decide to break up, give yourself some time before moving on to your new crush. You don't want to hop from one boy to the next. Take time to get to know your crush and find out if he's worthy.

### BREAKING UP IS HARD TO DO

I want to share with you what my mom shared with me after my first hard breakup. Okay, I was only 11, but at the time, it seemed like it was the hardest thing to go through. Anyway, the quote: "Since love is not a thing, it is not lost when given. You can offer your love completely to hundreds of people and still retain the same love you had originally." After going through it about a million times in my head, I realized she was right. I never lost love because I could still love people.

Breakups happen in different ways. You can be dumped, or you can be the one doing the dumping. You can find out directly or indirectly, like seeing your boyfriend holding hands with someone else (that is probably the toughest, I think). People break up by phone, by letters, or in person. No matter how it happens though, it hurts.

But even though he did the breaking up, I realized I am a good person and, if he can't realize that, he doesn't deserve me. I'm not conceited or anything, I'm just saying I don't want to like somebody who doesn't think much of me. So, I hung out with my friends more, participated in activities, and stayed involved at school. I even made a bunch of new friends. Believe me—it's great to be able to look at him and not feel sad anymore.

No matter what happens or how many breakups you go through, in time, you will get over it. I hope this helps you realize that even though breakups are tough, you will still have the love in your heart you had to begin with.

—Hadley G., 14

*Dear Lucky,*

*My boyfriend kissed my BFF. I can't dump him because I like him so much! And I can't be mad at my BFF because she didn't know he and I like each other. Should I dump him?*

*—Feeling Unsure*

She's your BFF, and she didn't even know you have a boyfriend? That is weird, but I guess you can't be mad at her if she didn't know. But you *can* be angry with him, unless there's a chance he doesn't know he's your boyfriend. If he does, there's no excuse for him kissing your BFF or any other girl. Even though you really like him, you might opt to move on. It sounds like you care a lot more about this crush relationship than he does.

# BONUS QUIZ:

## DOES BREAKING UP MEAN YOU CAN'T STILL BE BUDS?

*He broke up with you, and you're completely bummed out. You want to remain friends with him, but you're worried that he won't want to. Take this quiz to find out whether he could be a great bud, or if he wants to be left alone.*
—Danielle C., 12

**1. Before you fell head over heels, you were:**

a. friends forever.

b. friends of friends.

c. unaware of each other's existence.

**2. He thinks your friends are:**

a. cool girls. He doesn't mind you splitting your time with them.

b. total losers. He has a pet peeve about each one.

c. okay chicks. He'd rather hang with you alone, but once in a while he doesn't mind getting together with them, too.

**3. When you two broke it off, you felt like it was _____ in the room.**

a. ice cold. You're rightfully bitter because he dropped you for another girl.

b. warm. You were bummed, but you left on fairly neutral terms.

c. burning hot. His lame excuse left you steaming. This wasn't how you thought it would be.

**4. Your relationship lasted:**

a. one month. You both decided it wasn't working.

b. three months. You both changed and decided to go your separate ways.

c. six months. The whole thing ran its course.

**5. While you were together, he showed his affection by:**

    a. blowing you kisses between every class.

    b. holding your hand while walking you to next period.

    c. saying "hi" to you occasionally in the hallway. (Bonus points if he said "hi" in front of his pals.)

**6. For the anniversary of your first month together, he:**

    a. brought you flowers. You dried them and hung them up.

    b. forgot. Oops!

    c. made you a cute card with a simple "Happy Anniversary from Joe" written on the inside.

**7. Since you broke up two weeks ago, you've spoken to him:**

    a. only once. He called to see how you were doing.

    b. three times. It's hard not talking to someone you miss.

    c. every night. He can't decide if he really meant to break up.

**8. His friends:**

    a. still say "hi," but you know it's just to be nice.

    b. have spread rumors about the breakup to make you look bad.

    c. treat you the same as always. Just because you and your ex-crush aren't together, it doesn't mean you can't be their friend.

**9. Your 'rents are:**

    a. glad to see him go. They never liked him anyway.

    b. sad. He was nice to you.

    c. okay with it. As long as you're happy, that's all that matters.

**10. Your shrine of him inside your locker recently has:**

    a. been torn down, but not until you took a black marker and drew devil horns on his image.

    b. not moved. You can't stand the thought of taking it down.

    c. been dismantled, except for your favorite picture of the two of you together.

# SCORING

1. a. 3, b. 2, c. 1
2. a. 3, b. 1, c. 2
3. a. 1, b. 3, c. 2
4. a. 3, b. 2, c. 1
5. a. 1, b. 3, c. 2
6. a. 2, b. 1, c. 3
7. a. 2, b. 3, c. 1
8. a. 2, b. 1, c. 3
9. a. 1, b. 2, c. 3
10. a. 1, b. 2, c. 3

### 10 to 16 points: Leave Him Alone
Although this guy seemed great when you two were together, your breakup has most likely left you a little bitter and put out. Leave him behind, and move on. Or, better yet, learn to be happy by yourself. Who needs this guy? This one certainly isn't worth the effort.

### 17 to 23 points: Take It Slow
Hanging out together as friends might actually work for you two. Even though you might be upset about the breakup, you'll get over it in time. He may be upset, too, so give it time to heal. But it's possible for you to still be friends after the initial shock of the breakup wears off.

### 24 to 30 points: He's a Keeper
This guy obviously wants to be your pal. He was a good BF and deserves a second chance at friendship. You might find it awkward hanging out at first, but you care about each other. And kids who care (boys or girls) are the best friends to have.

# CHAPTER 6

# YOU SAID IT! MORE ADVICE FROM GIRLS LIKE YOU

**Y**ou've already read some of the great advice in this book by girls who've handled certain situations in smart ways. So we're gonna give Lucky a little break in this chapter and bring you even more great real-life advice from real girls!

# BFF DILEMMAS

Friendships are great! But things can't always run super-smooth between you and your BFF. We've rounded up some BFF dilemmas we hear girls complain about most often, and then we got real girls to give you their takes on how to handle these sticky friendship sitches. One girl's advice about a certain situation might be totally different from another's, so you get lots of viewpoints and can go for whatever works best for you.

*My BFF is jealous because I have a boyfriend. How can I make my friend understand that it's not my fault I have a BF and she doesn't—without hurting her feelings?*

**—Concerned Pal**

First of all, you can't take time away from your BFF. You have to show her that she is still an important part of your life. Also, assure her that someday a great guy will see how special she is!

*—Emily, 14*

Tell your friend how unfair it is for her to lay a guilt trip on you for having a boyfriend. But don't say anything that could be taken the wrong way.

*—Elise, 13*

Remind your bud there will always be times when you have a BF and she doesn't, and vice versa. Of course, you'd have to ask her first, but why not set her up with her own crush?

*—Paige, 13*

Sometimes, girls feel inferior if they're BF-less, but that's really wrong. So remind her what a great friend she is and that she'll probably have her own boyfriend soon enough.

*—Rebecca, 14*

Be sure to spend time just with her so she doesn't get jealous of the time you spend with your BF. Also, include her in some of the plans you make with your BF, and introduce her to his cute friends!

*—Katherine, 12*

> *My BFF moved away two months ago. We promised we'd always be BFFs, but she hasn't written at all! I've written her several e-mails, but haven't gotten a single response.*
>
> **—Empty Mailbox**

Your BFF has probably made new friends, and so should you. Also, write another e-mail asking for her phone number. Call her to talk. She probably isn't doing this on purpose. Give her time to adjust.

*—Taylor, 12*

She probably needs time to settle into her new home. I'm sure your BFF still wants to be friends. She might be busy adjusting. Also, remember e-mails can be case sensitive, so double-check to see if you have the correct address.

*—Kaitlyn, 12*

My BFF moved away, and we still keep in touch. We take turns calling each other every weekend, and we try to get together during the summer. Staying in touch is still hard for us, so maybe that is why your BFF hasn't responded yet. Keep trying.

*—Emily, 14*

I'm sorry your BFF does not return your e-mails. There are a number of reasons why she might not be writing back. Maybe there's something wrong with her computer. Even if she's not writing back, she probably still enjoys reading e-mails from you.

*—Ashley, 14*

Not answering your e-mails doesn't mean she doesn't want to be friends. Give her space to make new friends and get used to her new home. Then, write again. If she still doesn't contact you, maybe she's not a great friend after all!

*—Claire, 12*

You have the right idea about confronting your BFF. If she is really a good and true friend, you should be able to be honest and open about your feelings. Tell her the truth about how you feel, and let her know you don't want this to ruin your great friendship!

*—Caroline, 11*

Crushes are natural, so don't embarrass her by confronting her. Try to distract her instead by planning one-on-one activities that don't involve your brother. Go shopping, or check out a new girly flick together. This way, you can still see her and have fun—but she won't be hanging out with you just to see your brother.

*—Hayley, 11*

If your BFF really likes your brother, then you can't necessarily do anything about it. Look at the bright side—if she and your big bro get married some day, then she won't just be your BFF, she'll be your sister-in-law!

*—Brianna, 12*

Nicely explain your feelings to your BFF. Let her know how much this bothers you and how hurt you are. It is important to confront her by being honest and, if she values your friendship, she'll understand.

*—Samantha, 11*

Tell your BFF how you really feel. If your brother is a lot older than she is, tell her in a nice way that you are looking out for her and that she should find a crush closer to her age. Hopefully, she'll thank you for being such a great friend!

*—Megan, 12*

> *My crush and I have never been on a real date. But, we talk a lot. Isn't he off-limits to my BFF? They've been flirting with each other an awful lot, and it bugs me!*
>
> **—Claiming the Boy**

Does your BFF realize how important your crush is to you? Have a heart-to-heart, and explain to her how you feel about him. If she doesn't back off, decide if your crush or your friendship is more important. Maybe she's not your BFF after all.

*—Jaclyn, 11*

Talk to your friend, and make sure she knows the deal with you and your crush. Chances are he's a player, and, if she wants to remain a friend, she should step off.

*—Dara, 11*

Explain to your friend how you feel about your crush. It might not change her feelings for your crush, but at least you'll get your feelings across. Then, go for a different guy. There are tons of guys who wouldn't get between friends.

*—Leslie, 14*

Tell your friend how you feel about everything. Ask her how she'd react if you were to flirt with her crush. Let her know you're still her friend but that she needs to be more considerate of your feelings.

*—Alyson, 12*

Maybe your friend doesn't know you really like him. Definitely talk to her about it. Maybe there is a misunderstanding. A good friendship shouldn't be lost over a mix-up. Even if you are upset, you should never lose a good friend over a guy.

*—Angie, 12*

*I confronted a friend because my BFF says she dissed her, and the girl denied it. How do I get to the bottom of it?*

**—In the Middle**

Whatever you do, don't get anyone else involved. Try to remain neutral until you get an honest answer. If things worsen, remember that true friends don't lie to each other.

*—Kaitlyn, 11*

Get details from each friend, like who said what to whom. Once you know more about what happened, it'll be easier to move on. Tell your friends you don't like it when they bicker, and remind them that friends are honest with each other.

*—Amanda, 11*

Ask each friend what was said. If they are true-blue buds, they will be up-front with you. Just try to trust your friends as best you can.

*—Natalie, 11*

Talk to both friends at the same time, and try to get them to work out situation. Let them know friendships are really important to you, and that dissing each other isn't cool and upsets you.

*—Danielle, 12*

Invite them both for a sleepover, and ask them about the dissing. Tell your friends you just want the truth. You could add that maybe they could try to get along since they're both your good friends.

*—Shawna, 13*

*I had a sleepover, and my BFF hit it off with my sister. Now, my friend calls to talk to my sister and hangs out with her instead of me! I feel like my BFF totally ignores me now when I'm around.*

**—Left Out**

Ask your BFF why she chooses to hang out with your sister and exclude you. Invite her to do something, just the two of you—like go to the mall or just talk.

*—Alyssa, 12*

It's disrespectful of your BFF to ignore you. Maybe she doesn't realize she pays more attention to your sister. She probably thinks everything is okay and might not notice you feel bad. Let her know how you feel.

*—Alexa, 11*

Ask your friend why she's suddenly hanging with your sister and ignoring you. Tell your BFF—and your sister—you feel excluded. You'll feel better knowing what they think. Once you know, decide if your friend is worth the trouble.

*—Caley, 13*

Confront both your friend and your sister. Not in a mean way, but tell them you feel left out. If your sister is nice, she'll understand. If your friend is true-blue, she'll also understand.

*—Natasha, 13*

Suggest that the three of you hang out together. Also, tell your friend how you feel. If she's a true BFF, she'll work it out with you.

*—Elizabeth, 15*

> *My BFF and I aren't in any of the same classes this year, so I never see her. I feel lost without her! How can we stay friends?*
> —*Miss My BFF*

Look on the bright side. Here's your chance to meet other people and make new friends. You'll still miss your BFF, so try to spend time together on the weekends. Go to the movies, or just catch up on what's happening with each other.

—*Lan, 12*

You don't have to be in the same classes to stay friends. Call and e-mail each other! Have sleepovers, make a date for pizza, and/or meet up after school. Just think how special your get-togethers will be. In the meantime, try to make some new friends.

—*Carrie, 11*

Get together with your bud after school, and grab a bite to eat. If you are true friends, time apart shouldn't compromise your friendship. If you can't meet up regularly, chat over e-mail until you can.

—*Arella, 14*

I'm lucky because I have a phone in my room, so I call my BFF every day after school to ask how her day was and talk about our weekend plans. It's hard not always seeing my BFF but, when I talk to her, I feel happy and get a big smile on my face!

—*Courtney, 11*

I have the same problem with my BFF, and we've been friends since kindergarten! I talk to her in the halls, and we do things on weekends. Talk on the phone, and join after-school activities together. It's hard but, it's worth it!

—*Audrey, 13*

> *Aaargh! My BFF totally copies me. How can I help her develop her own style and personality without hurting her feelings?*
>
> **—Copied Gal**

Tell her nicely, "I know you like how I dress, but I'd appreciate it if we could dress differently." Be nice. Don't ruin the friendship. But if she's a toxic, cling-on friend, break it off. Just tell her you don't want to be friends anymore.

—*Thalia, 13*

It's not easy to be yourself and be a leader. So confront your BFF and tell her you appreciate her looking up to you but that you can't always be around to guide her. She needs to be her own person.

—*Lauren, 14*

It's important for everyone to feel accepted. Let her know you would like her even if she didn't like the same clothes or boys as you do. Being yourself is an important thing, but it is a really hard thing to do.

—*Allie, 14*

Let her know you don't appreciate it when she copies you. Tell her to find her own inner beauty because you know it's there. She should let her own light shine and not take it from someone else.

—*Paige, 12*

Take her shopping and show her cool clothes that you don't have. Hint to her how individual you try to be. She probably has good intentions and looks up to you. Tell her how you feel, and help her find her own style.

—*Grace, 13*

> *How can I go on vacation with one bud when another BFF invited me to go away, too? I don't want to hurt anyone's feelings.*
>
> *—Torn*

I wouldn't want to hurt either of my BFF's feelings. I would tell them both that I'm really sorry but that I can't go on vacation with either of them because I already have plans with my own family.

*—Barbara, 13*

If you've already been on vacation with one, go with the other one this time. If you haven't gone to either person's vacation place, go with the friend you'd have a better time with.

*—Gillian, 11*

I'd ask my parents which family they're most comfortable with me going on vacation with. Then, I would think about which friend I would have more fun with. Even though you're BFFs, you might be more comfortable around one friend's family.

*—Amanda, 12*

Tell them both you have plans with your family. Spending time with your family is better than rejecting anyone's offer. But before anyone packs their bags, have a bon voyage party with all your BFFs!

*— Sarah, 14*

You should go with the girl who asked you first. Tell the other BFF you'll make it up to her, and then do something special—like plan a cool one-on-one weekend together.

*—Julie, 13*

# YOUR BEST IDEAS EVER!

Here's some advice *Girls' Life* readers dole out. What follows are great ideas we've received from girls who really know how to make the best of any situation. No problems here....

## FRIEND MAKER

When meeting a new bud, the most important thing of all is to be yourself. Don't try to be someone you're not. Just have fun. Don't worry about whether you've found it hard to make friends in the past. Just think about all the friends you're going to have in the future!

—Sasha G., 13

## JOIN...UM...START THE CLUB

French Club and Future Teachers of America are fine for some girls, but they just don't cut it for you? So start your own club! What are you into? Writing? Collecting? Skating? Crafts? Or how about a club with a cause—neighborhood cleanup or visiting nursing home residents?

Whatever you go for, your club needs members, so tell your friends and tell them to tell their friends. Post flyers at school. Announce your club's startup and attach a sign-up sheet, asking for names, phone numbers, and e-mail addresses. Once you have a list of kids, pick a place to meet (backyard fort, club basement, park, or maybe the principal will let you meet in a classroom after school). Contact everyone with the meeting time—say Tuesdays from 4 p.m. to 5 p.m.

The main part of any club is to plan fun stuff you can do together. So at your first meeting, come up with a list of ideas and get the club members to vote on your first group activity. Your writing club could start out with haikus and progress to short stories. You want to cheer up the elderly? Make goodie baskets. Have one person make transportation arrangements, and put another person in charge of selecting things to go inside the baskets. Each club member can volunteer to do a different task to help make the activity happen. Most important of all? Have fun!

—Christie M., 13

## STAND UP FOR YOURSELF!

Last year, my friend suddenly changed over the summer. She avoided me, and if any other girls tried to talk to me, she told them I was a loser and not to be friends with me. My days were awful. Sometimes, I even cried. My mom said if I wanted it to stop, I would have to stand up to her. I was like, "Oh, easy for you to say. You don't have to put up with her!" But I found the courage. Next time she was mean to me, I ignored her. Surprisingly, she stopped being so mean! I guess when she didn't get a reaction from me, she got bored with it.

The first step to standing up for yourself is knowing you don't have to go through it alone. Talk to parents, relatives, friends, and guidance counselors. But they can't solve your problems. You have to take action! Here's how:

✿ First, try completely ignoring the person tormenting you. You don't see her, hear her—nothing!

✿ If ignoring your so-called friend (or ex-friend) doesn't work, try the rational approach. In a strong voice, say, "Why are you doing this?"

✿ Another idea: Don't give a social bully anything to work with—steal her thunder. When she teases you, try agreeing with her and laughing about it. What can she say?

✿ If all this advice fails, ask an adult to help work things out. And if anyone threatens you physically or hurts you, you need to tell someone right away.

—Brittany B., 14

## STAYING IN TOUCH OVER THE SUMMER

Have you ever had a hard time keeping in contact with your buds over the summer? Or gotten sick of writing six notes to six friends that say exactly the same thing? I have. So I started a newsletter for my buds, and here are some easy steps for making your own:

❀ *What do ya want in it?* Do you like sports? Jokes? Recipes? I put in secret codes with a decoding key.

❀ *Pick a title.* I chose *Always Friends*.

❀ *Do a little research.* Scribble down some jokes, make a puzzle, write an article.

❀ *Start workin'.* If you have a computer, then you're set. Make the title large at the top of the page. Include the date. Give articles catchy headlines. Remember good old sentence structure. Check spelling. When finished, print out as many copies as you need.

❀ *Decorate!* Grab markers, crayons, stickers, stamps, and colored pencils. Add pictures to go with articles, or just doodle.

❀ *Send 'em!* Make sure to close the envelope tightly, slap on a pretty stamp, and write the address clearly on the front. Or, you can send it via e-mail if your pals will be checking e-mail over the summer. Design your page using cool graphics and colors.

—Emily L., 12

## Eight Things to Do and Not to Do Around Your Crush

**8.** Never talk about your ex-crush! Big mistake.

**7.** Don't try to avoid him when walking down the halls at school.

**6.** Stay calm, and try not to be tense.

**5.** Flirt, a little.

**4.** Start a convo about something he's into.

**3.** Don't pretend to like all the things he likes, when you really can't stand them. Trust me—it will backfire!

**2.** Don't ignore him just because other people are around.

**1.** Be yourself! Don't try to be someone you aren't.

—Daniella, 13

## Battling for the Same Boy

Does one of your friends have a crush on the boy you like? The way I see it, you can choose one of three approaches when this happens:

**1.** Tell her you have a crush on him and that he is off-limits. This only works if you had a crush on him first, and she knew about it.

**2.** Tell her that since you both like him, you should agree that neither of you will get together with him. That way, no one gets hurt.

**3.** Let him decide who he likes, and be sure that there are no hard feelings for the person who isn't chosen. If the decision is his, you can't blame each other.

—Kimberly D., 13

# NINE WAYS TO IMPROVE YOUR GRADES AND STILL HAVE A SOCIAL LIFE

Sometimes, it's not easy to balance school responsibilities and just-wanna-have-fun time. These tips have really helped me out.

1. Keep an assignment notebook. List all your classes, and leave lots of room to write down your assignments and due dates. Check off each thing as you do it.

2. Keep an organized schedule, and follow it. Don't delay the dreaded things, and do the most important things first. The relief of having a tough job out of the way gives you more energy for other stuff.

3. Always do the thing that is due the earliest first. That way, if you don't get everything done, you're still in good shape.

4. Use your study hall time wisely, not chatting with a friend. It will be more fun when you and your friend get together later—you'll have your work done!

5. Keep organized! Put everything in its place, and you will save time hunting for it.

6. Do the best job in the simplest way. For example, when coloring a map for social studies, use light shades. It will be neater and more legible.

7. Ask teachers to update you on your progress. If you need to catch up, you can ask for extra credit work.

8. Reward yourself! After receiving an A, make plans to do something fun. And tell your parents you've worked hard and deserve praise.

9. Stay motivated! Wanting to get something done helps you along. The sooner you get your work done, the sooner you can do fun activities with your best friends.

—Rachel D., 14

# How I Solved Our Friendship Triangle

Colleen and I have been friends for almost a year and a half now. When we first met, we hardly ever argued. The times we did, we fought at lunch and forgave each other by the end of the school day.

After a year or so, Colleen became friends with a girl I didn't like because she made fun of me almost every day. So, I got angry with Colleen. I thought she would not want to be my friend anymore because her new friend would be a big influence on her. I decided to dump her before she could dump me. I didn't realize how stupid that was of me until I told my mom what happened.

"You don't have the right to choose who Colleen is friends with," my mom told me. She was right. I wrote a letter of apology to Colleen. I tried to sincerely explain what had happened from my point of view—what my feelings were and how I had dumped her out of fear. By writing it out, I was able to put what I was thinking into words, which I wouldn't have been able to do if I had tried to explain my feelings out loud.

At the end of my letter, I taped a friendship ring and wrote, "If you forgive me, wear this ring." I saw her wearing it during a group project in English the next day. That letter not only patched up our friendship, but it also strengthened it. I can't say the note had any effect on the girl I didn't like. Although we never became good friends, we can stand each other now, and she doesn't make fun of me anymore.

—April S., 13

# SHOP 'TIL YOU DROP

I have a great idea for any styling girl out there on a budget, or any girl who loves to shop and have fun! Every Saturday morning (well, not every...but most), my friends and I go junkin'. We hit rummage sales, thrift stores, and the dollar store at the mall.

On Friday night, we buy a local paper and look for all the Saturday garage sales. We write them all down on a list with times and locations. If there are any addresses we don't know, we look them up on a map ahead of time. Then Saturday morning, we grab some juice and some muffins, and off we go!

You name it, we find it! Usually, we have a price range of what we are willing to pay for certain things. For example, we usually pay between 5 cents and 2 dollars for a pair of jeans. I'll pay 25 cents to 50 cents for a paperback book, and 50 cents to 1 dollar for a hardback. Sometimes, you can offer less than what sellers are asking for something and they'll take it.

Yes, I know the stuff has been worn before. But hot water and a few runs through the washer always work to kill cooties. Seriously, think about all the people who try on clothes before you buy 'em. How uptight can you be after you think about that?

And believe me, when you add up how much you can save to spend on other things, you'll be amazed. Learning to sew is another great saver. I'm not talking about whipping up Calvin Klein outfits here—just learn enough to mend a seam, change buttons or shorten a skirt. I've patched up jeans and made them far cooler than anything store-bought.

It's really a lot of fun. One of the best things is, if I mess up any of these clothes, my mom doesn't get upset. After all, they didn't cost too much. When I'm older, I'd like to open up a clothes closet for the poor. I could buy clothes from garage sales, thrift stores, and the dollar store. I'll put them in my little store, but not charge one penny for anything. People who can't afford good clothes could come and shop for free. That would be so cool!

—Cherish W., 11

# How to Pass Notes in Class Without Getting Caught!

Esther:   One afternoon, my BFF Shayne passed by me nonchalantly and dropped a small folded piece of paper on my desk.

Shayne:   I wondered if Esther had gotten my drift to read the note, when I saw her foot next to me with a small piece of paper sticking out of her shoe. I took it.

Esther:   Next, I heard a long sigh as Shayne stretched her arms up behind her and dropped a crumpled note onto my desk.

Shayne:   We realized we had spent over 20 minutes passing notes and never got caught! So, we created more and more exciting ways to pass notes.

P.S.—Don't blame us if you get busted!

### Cannonball Pass
Write your message. Be sure your teacher is writing on the board. With extreme caution, crumple the note in a ball and throw it to your friend.

### Goody-Goody Pass
Ask your friend if you can see her notebook to catch up on the notes. Write your message on the margin of a piece of paper inside. Say, "Thanks, for the notes. Here's your notebook back." Give her a wink.

### The Football Pass (If your friend sits near you)
Write your message. Fold it in a rectangular shape. Place it halfway sticking out of the side of your shoe. Move your foot in front or behind you, and lightly kick your friend's foot to let her know about the foot message.

### Pen Pal Pass
Write your message. Fold your paper so it's really small and narrow. Place it in the cover of a pen. Casually say to your friend, "Here's the pen I borrowed." Give her a wink so she gets the hint.

### CHAIN GANG PASS
Write your message. Fold several times into a small square. Write "Please pass it on" on it. Cautiously hand the piece of paper to the person who sits next to you. If she isn't a goody-goody, she'll pass it along.

### NOTEBOOK BILLBOARD
Write your message on the front or back of your notebook. Raise the notebook to your eye level as if you're reading. Leave it this way for a minute or so, while your friend reads the message, then bring it back down.

### STRETCH PASS
Write your message. Crumple the note into a ball. Place the ball inside your hand and make a fist. Sit up straight, stretch your arms upward and make a yawning sound so the stretch seems real. Once your hand is up over your friend's desk, drop the note.

### TISSUE ISSUE (IF YOUR FRIEND HAS A TISSUE BOX)
Casually ask your friend for a tissue. Take out a tissue and write your "issue" on it. Fold the tissue back to its original form. Take out another piece of tissue and actually blow your nose, just to make the act seem real. Put the note-tissue back in the box and say, "Thanks, here's your box back." Give her a wink.

### SOCCER FIELD PASS
Write your message. Crumple it into a ball. Place it on the floor. When your teacher isn't looking, kick it over to your friend.

### FLY AWAY PASS
Write your message. Fold it into the shape of an airplane. When your teacher isn't looking, quickly fly the plane across the room to your friend. Warning: Be sure to have good aim.

—Shayne B., 11, and Esther L., 11

## No Boyfriend? No Problem!

Here are ten reasons girl friends are more fun than boyfriends.

1. Slumber parties—no boys allowed!

2. Girl friends will listen to your probs non-stop.

3. They are more fun to shop with.

4. Makeover parties!

5. You can hang out and do magazine quizzes.

6. You can swap clothes.

7. Girl friends don't break up with you.

8. They talk on the telephone for more than five minutes at a time.

9. You can act as silly as you want around girl friends.

10. You can talk about all your crushes.

—Megan R., 14

# PARTING WORDS: A NOTE FROM LUCKY

As you can see, we girls have a lot to learn from each other! I hope all the info in this book has shown you that you're not the only one facing the issues you face. I hope, too, that my advice has answered some of your questions and helped you learn more about yourself.

Life can be challenging at times. That's why we girls need to stick together. Remember that, when life gets you down or you just need to vent, you can always talk to your friends. That's what they're there for!

Look for additional advice in the pages of *Girls' Life Magazine*, where I'll keep tackling more tough dilemmas. Until then, here's my last bit of advice: Live your life to the fullest, and try not to let the little things get you down!

*Your Friend,*

*Lucky*